The Learner

The Learner

Confronting God, Golf, and Beyond

A Novel By

Thomas Franklin Warren

RESOURCE *Publications* · Eugene, Oregon

THE LEARNER
Confronting God, Golf, and Beyond

Resource Publications
An Imprint of Wipf and Stock Publishers
199 W. 8th Ave., Suite 3
Eugene, OR 97401

www.wipfandstock.com

PAPERBACK ISBN: 978-1-5326-5137-3
HARDCOVER ISBN: 978-1-5326-5138-0
EBOOK ISBN: 978-1-5326-5139-7

Manufactured in the U.S.A.

They learn from God, kids do, but also from golf. Kids of all ages.

Contents

Preface

THIS IS A STORY of a young man fresh out of seminary who becomes the pastor of a church seeking a new leader. Somebody, they advertised, ". . . who can relate to young people. Somebody who can offer us creativity. Somebody who can take criticism. We want somebody who likes challenges and is a great preacher. We are still learning about lots of things, and we hope that our new minister is too, but it wouldn't hurt if s/he is also a miracle worker."

The man who got the job was still learning, and he knew something about miracles. He had been part of one on a golf course. It hooked him on the game forever. So, when the church called him, they confronted something new with the golf, but challenges as old as the scriptures emerged as well: homelessness and love.

Introduction

THE VISITOR SAID, ". . . and they'll make you sign statements where you pledge to behave."

Everyone chuckled. One of the seminarians replied, "Tell me more."

"Well, congregations vary, but my first church was very clear up front that their clergy better not get into–they called it–a complicated relationship with a member. It might diminish one's objectivity as a spiritual leader."

The other visitor chimed in, "Yeah, that's chapter and verse for many churches. Even if they are two consenting adults, a pastor's primary relationship is to the parishioner, and it must be maintained. As a trusted mentor, not a friend or business partner or lover, or part of a member's regular golfing foursome."

Chris interrupted, "Even in congregations *led by our Chicago graduates*? Won't they be tolerant? Won't they treat us as individuals? The churches that hire us?"

"Some are very strict. They say that if the pastor-member relationship is no longer primary, then it needs to be severed in order for the parishioner to find a new spiritual leader. She or he may even have to stop attending that church."

Twelve first-year students and two ordained alums had gathered in what was known as the Lower Room, a relaxing place for libation and conversation in the basement of a big, old, white frame house in the cluster of seminary buildings adjacent to the University of Chicago campus. Its bulletin boards were plastered with notices of upcoming events and things for sale. Photos under the heading of "Trouble Makers" plastered the walls: Mother Teresa, Reinhold Niebuhr, Martin Luther King, Martin Luther, John Dewey, Jane Adams, Dietrich Bonhoeffer, and Mahatma Gandhi all stared right back at you. In a space labeled "Image of the Month" was a glossy black and white print of a homeless guy dozing in a sleeping bag curled up at the bottom of a south side street sign. "This could be Jesus," was scribbled on the wall next to the picture. Following it in a different hand: "Duh, no kidding."

These aspiring ministers of God were tapping into the experiences of two ordained graduates of the seminary who were back in Hyde Park for a conference about the future of Christian youth in mainstream America, but the topic of the moment was dual roles.

The first alum went on, "The simplest way to understand dual roles is that it's a conflict of interest. Parishioners' needs must be protected and come first. There was a minister's covenant or code–or whatever they call it–that I signed at the time of my ordination. It says that I will not use my ministerial status, position, or authority knowingly to misguide, negatively influence, manipulate, or take advantage of anyone in any way."

Chris gasped, "Wow, not *anyone?*" and everyone laughed, but he didn't think it was funny. Recently, he had dreamed of holding forth from his pulpit while a member who would become his future wife stared up at him from her pew.

The second alum said, "Without communicating clear boundaries up front, dual roles can become hard to manage, and harm a lot of people . . ."

Students interrupted.

"Can't congregations and clergy create their own special agreements? Ones that are mutually sensitive and respected?"

"What if they're not a member of the church–the other party? Does that make a difference?

"What about relationships with young people, like teenagers in confirmation?"

"It better be platonic."

"Or intellectual."

"Hey, even intellectual ones can cause trouble if they go in certain directions or too far. Be careful."

"What about sports? What if you like one team and they like another?"

The first alum spoke up. "Well, that's usually all in fun, but it, too, can go too far. Emphasizing sports. *Ad nauseum.* Pardon the image, but talking about sports is a lob shot or gimme putt for many ministers: Easy and irresistible. But be careful. Don't be known primarily as an athlete who came to The Lord, even if it's true."

The second alum added, "All of this is especially dicey if you are an unmarried pastor in a small town, since many people that you meet are either current members or potential ones, assuming you covet new acquaintances like most of us shepherds do."

A student went, "Baaa, baa." Only a couple of the others smiled.

"Hey, sports are important to lots of people. Too important, I think in many cases, but this never gets written into pledges about behavior, and please don't get me going on and on about Sunday morning soccer games and how they suck kids out of churches."

These topics were not new to Chris and his classmates, but talking about them in a group that included ordained clergy was sobering affirmation of what they had learned here and there: Being a minister of God is complicated and challenging.

Learning

The Call

CHRISTOPHER HILDING EK DIDN'T show early signs of becoming a minister of God. As a child, he wasn't one of those prodigies who wow the congregation from the pulpit by reading scripture with pre-pubescent self-possession. As a young teenager he attended confirmation classes, and when the time came he was welcomed into adult membership, but then his attendance plummeted and members who saw him around town would ask, "Where have you been?" As a high school student, he kept quiet about social issues-of-the-day and didn't join groups that had young progressive Christians all excited; but at a congregational event for high school graduates, a pillar-of-the-church took him aside and said, "You should become a pastor. You'd be good at it. I think you have character."

Chris stammered, "Well, thank you. I don't know about that one." Years later he wondered if that may have been the day a seed was planted, but at the time he had never considered the clergy as a vocation for himself or anybody, and he certainly didn't think of himself as having character.

The fall after high school he entered a small Midwestern denominational liberal arts college and learned that when his parents' and grandparents' generations were students there, they had to take religion courses, no matter what their majors or convictions. He didn't like that. *How ridiculous: forcing it on them,* but he decided to learn more. A passage from an old catalog he dug out of the college archives said:

"To graduate, students must earn credit from at least four courses that focus on issues that define and celebrate religion in this, our Christian nation." A few years later more wording had been added: "The fact that we require this foundation is *reasonable and proper.*" During the same era, those three words defined the speed limit in Iowa, just across the big river.

The college didn't mandate religion courses during Chris's time there, but it continued offering some that would have counted under the old rule: Ethics, Religions of the World, Old and New Testament Studies, American Denominationalism, Renaissance & Reformation, and others that would pop up from time to time. During his second semester Chris enrolled in one called The Philosophy of Subjective Culture. He always remembered how Professor Helms closed one of his lectures saying, "When I want to get control of a day that finds me too full of myself, I walk to the old cemetery near where I live and contemplate the worlds that are buried there. But any cemetery will do. Try it sometime. Please."

Chris did. Later that day and many times throughout his life.

During the first semester of his sophomore year Chris elected a course that was called Social Sources of American Denominationalism. A visiting German professor challenged students to analyze how various breeds of institutionalized worship formed and evolved in the United States. Chris had entered the course highly critical of the racial and social class homogeneity that characterized congregations of his grandparents' and parents' churches. He knew that back then on Sunday mornings the houses of worship were the most segregated places in America. "*Good God,*" he thought, "*why did those Swedes and Italians and Irish and African-Americans have to stay isolated to worship what they say is the same God.*" He cringed at that demographic at the start of the class, but wasn't so sure at the end. He had been exposed to the idea that leadership and candid expression flourished within racial and ethnic groups that were together with their own on the Sabbath. Separate from "integrated, diverse" sanctuaries controlled by white America.

Chris chose psychology as his undergraduate major. He liked its focus on individuals. "*Psych's all about me!*" he sheepishly admitted to himself. He also appreciated that psychology was interdisciplinary. Biology, computing, philosophy, economics, education . . . they all cut across psychology or maybe it was the other way around. When Chris suggested to Prof. Helms that everything is psychological because it all filters through the self, the wise man said, "I think everything is philosophical, and there's a person over there in the science building who thinks everything is geological. Think about that!"

When Chris wondered what he was going to do with life after college, something in the cognitive sciences became a natural choice, and the autumn after getting his Bachelor's degree, he entered a graduate clinical psychology program at the University of Illinois. Religion still had a hold on him. Sundays he would set out to sample local strongholds of Lutherans,

Methodists, Presbyterians, Unitarians, Baptists, and Congregationalists in the Champaign-Urbana area. He didn't think of it as worshipping. He was there to observe the ministers. Their behavior. Their messages. Their similarities. Their essences. Their quirks. What might attract him–or anyone–to them? Or not. Sometimes he thought he could do their job better.

During those raw, windy first semester autumnal days he soberly came to acknowledge two chilling conclusions: that his graduate psychology curriculum was relentlessly geared toward producing researchers–not the humanistic clinicians he identified with–and that none of the churches he visited fueled his inner fire.

In early November, he escaped to the University of Chicago and experienced a warm weekend that would change his life. A friend from undergraduate days, Robert LeRoy, was enrolled in Seminary there. Chris had anticipated playing chess and listening to classical music with Bob–and he did that–but before going back to the U of I to grind away, he turned down an opportunity to sample golf at the public course in Jackson Park.

"Come on, let's get in a quick nine," Bob said. "It's such a gorgeous day. It may be a last chance before the snow flies."

"Nah," Chris replied with some sharpness of tone. "I'm not a golfer. I don't plan to ever take up that game . . . of the rich, by the rich, and for the rich," but then it hit him that his grandparents loved golf. "*Hmmm. They aren't that rich and I love them. What do they know that I don't?*"

So, Robert LeRoy couldn't tempt his friend to sample the agonies and ecstasies of golf that day, but this fellow's enthusiasm and dedication to serious seminary studies led Chris down another path he never consciously intended to travel: toward the ministry. To his kith and kin, it appeared to be an impulsive move that should have been thought through long and hard, but Chris had been carefully considering vocations. He wanted one that helped others and gave him an opportunity to experience the fullness of life.

Bob and he talked long and hard about downsides of the ministry: You're working for so many bosses (in addition to God). You can get relocated to another parish against your will. The pay isn't good. While the stereotype has you working just on Sundays, in fact you are on the clock all day every day and night. It's not easy for a single person to find a love partner, because those in the congregation are off limits. Some members are holier-than-thou with no behavior of their own to back it up. Some members are saints, and you probably aren't. It's not easy.

They sighed and smiled. Then Bob said, "But I'm glad I took the plunge."

And Chris was convincing himself: "*I was cut out to be a minister long ago. Now's the time to act on it, here in Hyde Park.*"

He liked the people he met at the Chicago Theological Seminary and what their institutional rhetoric emphasized. All degree programs involved rigorous study of religion, a profound appreciation for diversity and inclusion, and the flexibility of a multi-vocal and multidisciplinary approach. Whether you are interested in parish ministry, counseling, social service, community organizing, teaching, or theological research, there was a CTS degree program capable of preparing you for your chosen pursuit. Christopher Hilding Ek saw these values in the students and faculty he met in Chicago. He left the University of Illinois after one semester and became a fresh new seminarian in January.

Eventually, he decided that he would focus his ministry on young people. Everyone he respected said that the younger generation is the future of the church and without a dynamic future, we are finished. Chris could identify with this warning. In his home church, most kids dropped out after confirmation and the remaining members kept looking older and older. And the church was with no easy replacements when they died, but he didn't think that young people got a chance to show what they could do. To strut their stuff. To fully become members.

Chris liked young people when he was one of them, and he liked the prospect of feeling young forever. Everyone said his mother was a kid at heart. He liked that. Young people–new people–can capture and run with so many wonderful zany ideas, if they're not squelched. Chris didn't hate many things, but he hated when young people's ideas were quickly criticized without a hearing. Without a patient attempt to look them over and at least say hmmm.

What convinced him that he could have success along these lines crystalized during a so-called field education experience. A seminary faculty member had taken him to a south side church that was about to give up trying to bring any new sheep into its dwindling flock, and briefly introduced "Mr. Ek" to a group of young people who were self-described as packing up to leave organized religion. In fact, they had strong attractions to their church: the stained-glass windows, the choir, the security of a Sunday morning, the adults who were so nice to them, and each other. In their hearts they didn't want to leave, but the place lacked energy, and it didn't turn them on spiritually. They felt squelched.

When the seminary guy left, Ek was alone with the kids. Avoiding small talk, he said, "I'm trying to learn to be a minister. When people know that and see you coming, all too often they change the subject. And then sometimes those very same people will later come into your office and tell you the most remarkable things. Amazing personal stuff that gives me goose bumps. There's a lot under the surface of life. A lot of malice and dread and guilt, and much loneliness, where you wouldn't really expect to find it, either. And some real joy."

The room went crypt-quiet. He waited, panning his eyes across their faces. Finally, he looked down and found a spot in a rumpled sheet of paper he was holding. He was about to try what he learned from a fascinating teacher in high school: Share something that means a lot to you. Something personal. Very quietly Chris read,

"Happy birthday flesh and bones. How does it feel to have another year go by? Last night I dreamed that these circles around the sun are wonderful weekends that fly by too fast (I was thinking of you). Slow down, earth. I want to take in the wonder of it all before falling asleep and dreaming. Isn't that strange? I have always told you I dream, but for heaven's sake, what do you think it means? This one. In case you haven't known this before I love you."

He stopped. The south side cynics before him stayed quiet for a full ten seconds, and then exploded with questions: "Who is that guy, the one talking? How old is he? Did you write it, or did some kid? You're just a kid at heart, aren't you?"

He said, "What do you think?"

They laughed together and talked on and on. Rising seminarian Christopher Ek brought things to a close by saying, "When we next meet–next week, same time, here–I want you to teach me something. I don't care what it is, but I want it to be interesting to you. Okay?" They stared at him. He went on. "When you teach–any of you–*you* learn the most. Your students might learn too, but you-the-teacher *will* learn. So, when we get together next time, I–your student–might learn. *You will learn.* Class dismissed." He hadn't even asked their names.

Ek had no idea if any of them would return or do the assignment, but they all came back. Prepared.

One of them taught about Illinois politicians who wound up serving time in prison: Republicans. Democrats. It didn't matter. She closed with, "What is there about Illinois that gives us this heritage?"

Another described what she called a pretend Catholic church with females as priests and popes, and a tradition of keeping males in secondary roles. She closed by saying, "I'm what they call a lapsed Catholic, but I wonder if I'd join it. The new church that I created."

Barack Obama's presidential library and the private police force at the University of Chicago were other topics that day, but the one that stuck with Chris the most was a description of a social media effort to encourage kids to become homeless. To choose to become homeless! The young person said, "I tried it! I did it, and I can see why people join ISIS or become suicide bombers."

The students were engaged, and the aspiring Pastor Ek didn't have to convince them that what they were starting to explore was important. And spiritual. One of them said it in those very words. Chris continued learning and worshiping with them during the rest of his time at seminary, and kept in touch with some down through the years including two students from South Africa. Both were children of faculty members at the university. One was a white Afrikaner, Roland Ruus; the other a black Xhosan, Themba Madiba. Prior to Chris's appearance, they were passively polite to each other, awkwardly co-existing. With him around they became fast friends and perceptive observers of their homeland from different vantage points. Later in life both credited Pastor Ek for providing the setting that brought them together for good.

Word got around about Chris's success with the youth. They were saying this guy from the seminary is cool. "He listens and he has a way of getting through to us. You can tell that he's sharing something that means a lot to him. He takes a chance that we might laugh at him, but we usually don't. Mr. Ek never tells us that he is going to do this and that, he just does it. He assumes we'll understand. He takes us seriously."

Chris's seminary classmates would stop by to watch him lead groups of teenagers. He made everyone participate. Their spirits were high and so were his. He was in the early stages of feeling his call to the ministry.

In One!

During an Easter break from seminary studies in Chicago, Chris visited his maternal grandparents in Florida. They lived at a place called The Villages, a retirement community near Orlando designed by, for, and dedicated to golfers. Chris had just come in the front door of their condo, put down his suitcase, and kissed G'ma when she held him at arm's length, flashed her gorgeous smile, and recited one of The Villages' favorite marketing lines: "This is the only place in the world where you can play golf free for the rest of your life!"

"Wow!" he exhaled, but before he could say more she linked their arms and pulled him outside where they slid into her electric golf cart and headed for a food mart on an asphalt path too small for cars but just right for her set of wheels.

"I've got a few things to pick up. Then I'll take you to G'pa. (She pronounced it Gee Pa.) He's dying to see you. He's out on the course somewhere.

Would you believe he's got a cart too?" she said while leaning through the curves and loving every minute touching shoulders with her grandson. After shopping, Grandma drove along one of the golf courses before screeching to a stop. She waved at some old guys getting ready to hit their tee shots on a par 3 hole. It was G'Pa with two of his pals.

G'pa's face lit up when he saw Chris. "C'mon, grandson, join us. We can both use my clubs, and you can ride with me." The others nodded.

Chris said, "You know I'm no golfer, Grandpa. I'd probably miss the ball entirely. Actually, I've never even played a hole, other than Mini-golf. Why don't I just tag along and watch you artists perform?"

G'pa said, "Aw, come on, kid. It's never too late to start, and I can't think of a better way for you clergy types to get away from the cares of the world for a while. Hey, you should take up the game. Start by playing with us right here and now. Don't worry about the bad shots. We hit them all the time, and we are very kind when one of us is struggling. Right, guys?" The others seemed to agree. *What happened next would stay with all of them for the rest of their lives.*

Ek chose Grandpa's seven iron, teed up a ball, took a couple of goofy practice swings, aimed at the hole, swung for real, and made a hole in one. This young man had not played golf, and his first shot was an ace. Many dedicated life-long linksters never experience this apogee of ecstasy.

As soon as the club met the ball Ek sensed he had hit it squarely. "Purely," he would eventually say in a sermon. It soared toward the center of the green with a little left to right drift. The flagstick was tucked into the back corner on what golf course architects describe as a shelf. The ball hit softly, rolled on an arc up the slope, clanked against the flagstick, and dropped into the hole.

To the dumbfounded three old witnesses standing on the tee box, here was a kid who had never hit a golf ball on a course, and he gets a hole in one on his first shot. It's Guinness Book of World Records stuff that probably never happened before in the history of the universe. A miracle.

One of them said, "Do you realize what you have done, and the pin is in the toughest position for that green." Christopher smiled sheepishly and shrugged.

Word spread fast on the course and beyond about the hole in one. Someone texted to The Villages' *Daily Sun* newspaper, and the story was on its way to going viral even before Chris was handed the obligatory bill tallying the "Free drinks for everyone!" that are expected in clubhouse bars when someone gets a hole in one.

G'pa paid.

During announcements Sunday morning at Grandma and Grandpa's church, Christopher was introduced as a visitor. The congregation broke into applause. They didn't do that for anything else that day. His golf feat had preceded him. He was a celebrity.

That—he called it miraculous—hole in one led to a closer relationship to his grandfather, to an appreciation of the seductive power of golf, and ultimately to a series of sermons about epiphanies, agonies, and ecstasies. Earlier Christopher Hilding Ek had apparently been called by God, and now by golf.

2

Challenges

Fair Are the Meadows

WHEN CHRIS TOLD HIS fellow University of Illinois psychology students that he was transferring to the Chicago Theological Seminary, one of them said, "You'll never get a job after you graduate. Pews are emptying and churches aren't hiring." But Chris got a job right away. In Belle Waters, Wisconsin, just north of the border with Illinois at Fair Are the Meadows Family Church. A key passage on line advertising their job description for a full-time minister read:

"We want somebody who understands us, who recognizes the modern dilemmas of ministry, and who can relate to young people. Somebody who can offer us creative leadership. Somebody who can take criticism. We want somebody who likes challenges. A great preacher and a miracle worker."

Chris chuckled when he first read it, but concluded, "*That's me*," and threw his hat into the ring. Early telephone conversations and his first visit to Belle Waters were positive. He felt comfortable with terms of the call which essentially said you need to do just about everything.

Eventually, he was asked to come to Belle Waters for face-to-face talk and what they called a site visit. He looked forward to it. He knew he knew his stuff and he felt comfortable knowing he wouldn't come across as a haughty know-it-all. Definitely not holier than thou. A friendly young mid-westerner.

Physically, Chris was sometimes affectionately described as a reincarnation of Huckleberry Finn: unkempt ginger hair, a crooked smile, and clothes that weren't a perfect fit. They were usually clean and new, but he would let the shirt tails hang out without realizing it, and his trousers hung very low on his narrow hips so his pants legs would slip along the ground after a while. Golfers might say he looked like the Hall of Famer Tom Watson casually dressed for a practice round with his old Kansas buddies. He was about Watson's size, five feet nine–if his shoes had thick soles and heels–with solid shoulders and strong arms. Chris wasn't unaware of how his body looked, and he could dress up when needed, but he was anything but a poser. Non-threatening.

For interviews or in new social situations he lived by the rule that it is better to be overdressed than too casual. For the face-to-face performance at Belle Waters he donned his most formal plumage: a dark grey suit complemented by a robin's egg blue shirt and a dark maroon tie. He made sure his black shoes were polished and his socks were plain grey.

So, Chris was selling himself, but the church was doing the same. They wanted to make a compelling impression on this young man who emerged as their first choice from a list of seven who all looked good on paper.

"How can we be at *our* best?" one member of the search committee asked others as they met to prepare for Chris's visit.

"Well, let's make this place squeaky clean for one thing."

"Let's give a history of the architecture of our building."

"Let's take him on a tour of all the good things that are happening along the river in Belle Waters."

"Let's just be ourselves," Joyce Ahlgren said and that turned out to be the last word before she led a prayer of hope for the future. And they adjourned with fingers crossed. Nobody suggested that Chris should meet with young people.

Conversations with candidate Chris went well. In one gathering where the search committee and he sat in a circle in the Riley Room to "get acquainted," a member asked,

"What makes you tick, Mr. Ek?"

Chris paused and everything was quiet for a time that was on the verge of becoming embarrassing. Then he said, "I'm still learning. I think I have something to offer, but wherever I wind up, I know that my friends in the pews will have a lot to teach me. Maybe more than I teach them. You. Whoops, I haven't been hired yet."

Everybody laughed.

The search committee of "Meadows" gushed with superlatives about Chris-the-candidate and recommended that the congregation vote to call him, but before closing the deal they needed to hear him preach. So, Chris returned to Belle Waters from Hyde Park and delivered a sermon he titled Hitching a Ride.

Instead of proceeding down the middle aisle to the front of the sanctuary at the beginning of the service–which was the tradition at Meadows–he stayed at the back until the organ prelude was over. With everything quiet and expectant, he called out in a plaintive voice "I need a ride. Please pick me up." All heads turned to the rear.

He was dressed in a ragged flannel shirt and dark green work pants. He had purposely mussed his hair. He dragged a beat up little suitcase on wheels and walked sideways down the aisle thumbing for someone to give him a lift–to help him. The congregation seemed confused, but one of them squeezed out of her pew and offered a hand. She pretended she had a car and told him to hop in. He did and they drove to the front. She dropped him off, and he unpacked his stuff.

It contained the gown and hood that he wore at the Chicago commencement–which he quickly put on–plus three books: *The Bible*, Marilynne Robinson's *Gilead,* and *Golf in the Kingdom* by Michael Murphy. He called them "Three friends who are always there."

Then he said, "Today I'll say some things as if I am your pastor. Of course, that is not true, yet. I pray that you will call me and if so, I will answer yes, but I realize that may not happen. You may decide to throw me out on my ear. [Congregational laughter] In any event, I begin with these words from scripture:

"From Gen 37:15. A man found him, and behold, he was wandering in the field; and the man asked him, 'What are you looking for?'

"From Ps 26:2-3. Examine me, O Lord, and try me; Test my mind and my heart. . .

"From Jas 4:13-15. Come now, you who say, 'today or tomorrow we will go into such and such a town and spend a year there and trade and make a profit,' yet you do not know what tomorrow will bring. What is your life? For you are a mist that appears for a little time and then vanishes. Instead you ought to say, 'If the Lord wills, we will live and do this or that.'"

He paused as if to say a little prayer in silence, and then began his homily. "Even if I get this job, I won't be with you for long. My time here will be short, but I hope it will have some sweetness." The members' eyes were wide, some with mouths agape like holes on a practice putting green waiting for balls to drop.

Then candidate Ek glided into the main message, which emphasized that all of us–like Jesus–are on earth for such a short time. He talked about possibilities and opportunities for that time. He shared an incident regarding one of his Chicago "kids," and then he sang a verse from the hymn that gave this Belle Waters church its name. In a pretty good baritone voice to the melody he associated with *Beautiful Savior.*

Fair are the Meadows, fairer still the woodlands,

Robed in the blooming garb of spring;

Jesus is fairer, Jesus is purer,

He makes the woeful heart to sing.

Chris appreciated that they didn't applaud. He said, "I love the name you have given your church, . . . our church?"

His sermon ended with, "To you young people in the congregation: when you are middle-aged or older and look back on what characterized Meadows Church during these precious times—now—it will seem like I stayed at Meadows for a long time, because it will have been for a big span of your adolescence. To you older friends sitting out there this morning—parents, grandparents, others: I hope that you think that my time with you sped by, because time flies when . . . well, when you're having . . . good times together. If I am so privileged to get this job, I hope my time with you will be enjoyable, and much, much more. I hope we can learn something together. Amen."

The people clapped long and strong.

After the benediction, members were instructed by the chairperson of Meadow's governing board to stay in the sanctuary for "our most important decision in years." Then he said some nice words about Chris who fielded softball questions before being excused so the congregation could vote on his call.

The yes vote was unanimous and he returned to the sanctuary greeted by a standing ovation. At a reception downstairs he was feeling so relaxed and expansive that he said, so everyone could hear, "Well, now I feel I can ask for something that I know you will understand: I like golf and want be out on the links quite a bit during my days off—my hours off? Is that okay?"

"Who said there would be *any free time?*" came a voice from the crowd gathered around him. Everyone laughed. Chris took that for a yes and breathed a sigh of relief.

He wasn't kidding about wanting time to play golf. While the hole in one in Florida dramatically captured Chris's attention, his subsequent attempts to see if he could consistently hit the ball showed promise. He could point to a memorable practice session that may have revealed that the ace wasn't just luck. At a humble driving range on the south side of Chicago he was going through wedges and seven irons that produced occasional lofted straight shots, but pathetic dubs and dribbles always followed them. With six balls left, he was ready to give up for the day when he grabbed his three metal, planted his feet about the width of his shoulders, and swung hard without any thought to mechanics. The ball rocketed off the clubface, and he felt that stretched completion of a full-release follow-through. He tried it again, and the same sensation rippled through his body: the sweetness of a shot hit squarely with nothing held back. He left the range euphoric and thought *I've found it. How to hit a golf ball.* In fact, Chris was doing something correct with those shots. His strong grip and flat swing plane working with legs placed just right gave him freedom and power. His backswing was smooth and his turn to the ball gave him club head lag into the hitting area. He didn't think about these particulars, he just swung away. But like all golfers, his hope of taking these successes from the range to the golf course, or even to his next practice session, were unrealized. He could not easily duplicate those pure shots the next time out, but the potential was there. It was in him. He would work to recover it. With pleasure. He was hooked.

After the vote of the congregation, the president of the board contacted regional offices of the United Church of Christ, Chris's ordination was conducted within a few weeks, and he was installed as Pastor of Fair Are the Meadows Family Church. The congregation offered him a housing allowance, which he used to rent a place near the Belle Waters College campus. Seminarian buddies in Hyde Park helped him load his stuff into a U-Haul trailer; members from Fair Are the Meadows were ready at the other end. Some things, like books, went into his church office; the rest into his new digs on the first floor of a house on Midwest Avenue.

A potentially awkward moment was avoided when someone asked, referring to golf clubs, "Where should these go?"

Chris really wanted these friends to reside in his office so he could fondle them as he checked out swing thoughts and contemplated congregational issues that he knew would come at him. He also suspected that if a Fair Are The Meadows member of Belle Waters Country Club spied them all lonely looking in a corner, a welcome invitation for lunch and eighteen holes may follow. But all of that may not look so good. The clubs in the office. He came to his senses and fibbed, "I've got to clear my mind of golf thoughts when I'm on the clock. Let's put them in the garage."

Of course, as a minister Chris would always be on the clock, and swing thoughts about golf always competed for attention with everything else, usually very successfully. He soon decided to bring a putter and seven iron to work and keep them near his desk as conversation pieces to be sure, but also to give him a chance to hone his short game skills. He would discover that transferring swing thoughts into action was like creating a sermon out of the flutters of life that caught his attention: Tantalizing and lined with hazards.

Clearly, Fair Are the Meadows got a shot in the arm when Christopher Ek became part of the family. The challenges that seemed so insurmountable when the search for a minister began were softened by his energy, his big smile, and the way they thought he would come across with young people. It was the beginning of a period of new hope.

Ek humbly acknowledged to himself that–along with Jesus of course–he was an embodied presence that exhaled this new spirit, but in spite of many fulfilling days and friendliness like he had never experienced, he soon began to feel the pressure of expectations. Some new trickles of acid in his stomach came from what the congregation wanted him to do; the rest flowed out of his developing sense of what the struggling little church had to offer him, or not.

Like, the condition of the building. It was what his mother would call pathetic. All the machinery that provided heating, cooling, and lighting needed updating. Vintage carpeting presented a threadbare trail where parishioners had walked to and fro for years. Dust was in corners and covered everything in unused rooms. He called these maintenance issues little errors of omission and wasn't overly concerned about them on their own, but when he learned about details of the financial situation of the church, he thought "*I should have learned more about this before I was hired,*" and when he witnessed bickering and occasional nastiness among members toward each other–"*I thought this group was above that sort of thing*–his burden became heavier.

He started worrying big time during his second month on the job, and soon he was having trouble getting to sleep at night and resting during the fitful times after he finally did drift off.

One dream found him halfway down the center aisle when some of the golf clubs fell out of their bag and echoed against the pews like hammers on an out-of-tune xylophone. He scrambled to put them back, but things got worse. He tripped–his golf shoe spikes got snagged by the carpet–and braced himself for the fall by grabbing the shoulder of a young woman sitting on the aisle. He hadn't seen her before, but she looked kind of familiar. A video recording of his dramatic entrance would show that he actually touched her in a way that some people would call indecently, but everything was happening so fast that people have to understand that he was just struggling to keep his balance. He reflected, "*Cameras can cause you troubles these days. Everyone has them,*" and he flashed back to when one of his Chicago students asked what would have happened to the emergence of Christianity if a camera had been there during Jesus' murder and–she cleared her throat–resurrection. 'Cameras don't lie, do they?'"

The organ prelude stopped in mid phrase, and the congregation went silent. "*Why don't they help me? I'm struggling.*" He had to keep moving toward the front of the church so he could stand in the pulpit and lead a dignified service, but with every step forward, the pulpit moved farther away. He stretched out for it, stumbled, and fell out of bed. He snapped awake all sweaty, but relieved when he realized he was home. *"What was that all about? It must have something to do with being behind schedule for preparing this Sunday's sermon. I should have had it wrapped up by now."*

But the whole past week had been brutal. The governing board meeting on Monday evening went way too long. The denominational gathering in Madison took up all of the second half of Tuesday, and website problems wiped out Wednesday. He could handle all that, but Thursday came from a very dark place. He said to himself. *"I like that woman. Mrs. Ahlgren. I still do. I think of her as a great person, but her criticisms? Ouch."*

The quality of his Friday golf added to his week of woes. He thought, *"My game sucks. I thought I was getting somewhere with those videos from Golf Channel, but three shanks and a bladed chip don't exactly give a guy confidence. I still could have broken 50. I missed two putts that should have gone in, and my tee shots took unlucky bounces. I was fascinated by that guy I got paired up with though. I can't remember his name. Interesting, I should never forget the name of somebody who might come to my church for the first time. On the golf course, I'm not myself. Too ego involved with how I'm doing. Gotta watch that. The guy looked like he could have been homeless.*

"Homeless. I'm still bothered by the tension–it was almost a shouting match–at the Monday meeting. I guess the church's homeless program–they call it Helping Hands–is a good idea, but Elder Holmstrom had a point: 'It's mainly to salve our consciences, not provide a long-range solution.' I heard him. Isn't it kinda like sending ready-to-eat meals periodically to people in need? Giving them fish instead of teaching them fishing?

"The answer seems like a no-brainer, but I guess it's not. It's not! On Monday night I was asking myself if any of us in the church would open our homes for a homeless person to come in and live there? Really do it. Even for just a few days. How many would? How many of my seminary buddies or professors would? Would I? (No). Jesus would. I'm sure he would. I think he did. What really gets me is that I didn't say anything after that awkward silence that got everyone hurling spears at each other. Somebody else had to change the tone that finally got us talking candidly. Damn. I've got to be a leader. Who cares who says what and who gets the credit? That meeting must have given me the nightmare, but it was a good one . . . the meeting."

The Magic Move

Rev. Ek loved to go places on foot. Anywhere. Anytime. As a kid, he walked his paper route when other kids rode bikes, he walked to school, and when he was in college, he took a job as a United States Postal Service letter carrier back home during summers and Christmases. Up and down porch steps all day. Good for the legs.

In keeping with that tradition on the golf course, he walked and carried his clubs. All fourteen of them, the maximum allowed. No motorized carts for Ek in spite of being the descendant of a pair of grandparents who owned two of them. One day he'll have to preach a sermon based on the messages at some American layouts. They say, *"Golfers on foot have no standing on this course,"* meaning you must use a motorized golf cart here. He could talk about those who have no standing in society. Or the problem of laziness. Or the treatment called exercise.

"I like to walk more than I like to pray, but maybe walking is praying," Rev. Ek had concluded to himself recently with a little smile.

He texted this preference to one of his seminarian buddies who fired back, "What do you like better, Master's Week or Holy Week?"

Chris equivocated with, "I think of them both as holy and sometimes they come at the same time."

Ah, the sweetness of walking. Tramping around the edge of the Belle Waters College playing fields with buds in his ears and friends named Renee Fleming and Doris Day and Frank Sinatra and Simon & Garfunkel and Judy Garland singing to him from places that had to be in heaven. Walking around other parts of town introduced him to the community. *"I love it when my legs feel strong and springy. And to do it with comfortable shoes that I don't ever think about when I'm out there. Hmm. I wonder why golf shoes were in that dream?"*

His favorite pedestrian route included the stretch along the east side of the Rock River north from downtown: the murals of industrial workers, the dam, the high school campus, the eagles. His heart beat faster as he turned east, climbed the hill alongside the library and continued on to the Neighborhood Community Center on Wright Street. "What a wonderful name for a place where I'm trying to learn."

Waiting for him is his teacher: A person who will guide him through the twists and turns of his journey through golf. He's called Keyshawn Gentry. A bit taller than Ek, he knows the game and those who play it. And he has his eye on the ones whose lives may turn out for the better if they would only take it up. Golf. At least that's what Rev. Ek was told by Sandy, the administrative assistant at Meadows Church, during his first week on the job.

"Mr. Gentry has a reputation as a golfing authority, and beyond," Sandy said. "He's kind of like a counselor, I guess. He has an office at the Community Center where he meets with neighborhood kids and their parents. He has built an enclosed golf practice area there where he retreats over the noon hour to hit balls. Kids watch him, and then he invites them into having a go. He hands them a club and encourages them to swing away. He's very positive about reacting to their first attempts. That's what I'm told anyway. He takes them as they are. He's patient. Would you like to meet him? I can put you in touch."

Chris said yes. He soon met with Mr. Gentry at the Center and after chatting about his new ministry and golf, he hit some practice balls under expert scrutiny. What Sandy said rang true. Mr. Gentry was encouraging and positive in critiquing Chris's swing. And he listened.

"May I take lessons from you?" Chris asked as their first meeting drew to a close.

"Of course. I will be pleased to work–learn–with you. All teachers are learners, you know."

So, once a week Chris would walk from church to his lesson.

There would be no warm-up small talk from Keyshawn Gentry, just a smile and a projection of quiet confidence as the man said, "Let's review from last time. Please describe the magic that is the key to everything we are working toward. And say it out loud like you're talking to a beginning golfer." He folded his hands in his lap and waited.

Being a professional wordsmith Rev. Ek feels comfortable in this role. "Okay, new learner," he said to an imaginary person wanting to do golf, "you have to bring the club to the top of your backswing very slowly. I can't over-emphasize this: really, really slow. Take a relaxed stance with your hands and arms hanging down naturally before you grip the club, and then start the backswing. S–l–o–w–l–y. Do everything slowly. Let your left heel come off the ground a little bit, rotate your body, and pull the club back to–do we call it parallel? (Keyshawn Gentry nodded.) Then still very, very slowly start your downswing by planting your left foot back on the ground, and after waiting a second or so, bring your right elbow slowly but firmly against your rib cage and pull down with a straight left arm."

Looking at Mr. Gentry, Chris was speaking reverently and fishing for compliments. "You told me to repeat this exercise many times, and I have, at home and at church in the privacy of my study."

Gentry almost broke into a smile and said, "Pretty good."

He had been trying to teach Ek what some serious golfers call the magic move, as described by golf teacher Harvey Penick in *The Little Red Book*. When mastered it generates increased body-arm torque. Club head speed follows, the key to hitting the ball a long way. It's not natural for many people–the magic move–but every excellent player does it, no matter what their swings look like from the outside (Okay, some don't raise their heel at all and during a real swing everything's faster). Rev. Ek would one day say from the pulpit: *"Learning the magic move was an epiphany for me. Do you have a magic move? Yet? In something that triggers action? It doesn't have to be in golf."* A few parishioners would raise their hands.

Finally, Mr. Gentry said, "Okay, now please show me," and he handed Ek a weighted club and stood back. "Okay. Not bad. But we have work still to do." Chris left feeling hopeful.

Crossing the State Line

Another favorite walk has Ek going south past the post office to the path paralleling the east side of the river. Sometimes it takes him a long time to get across to the other side of Stateline Avenue, and other times he doesn't get across at all if a certain guy is planted on the ground near the stop sign.

The first time Ek saw him, he walked right by. They avoided eye contact and he continued across Stateline, but the next time they acknowledged each other, and soon they were thumbs-upping back and forth when Ek was half a block away closing in from the north.

The guy was homeless. Usually alone, he liked the spot by the stop sign, a handy place to catch the eye of a motorist heading south and turning right. Who knows, it could lead to some cash or food. A home-cooked meal? A roof over his head? A friendship? He had cardboard signs asking for all of these things plus a prayer.

Ek learned stuff from the guy-by-the-stop-sign, who knew Belle Waters and a lot more. Ek would ask him questions and he would fire back with ones of his own. Very similar to those Ek still chews on with his seminary buddies: Why are we in this world? What is a real friend? Who is really responsible for homeless people? . . . Like me? the guy-by-the-stop-sign once asked]. Ek responded, *"Let me think about that,"* and then couldn't think about anything else during the rest of his walk. Sometimes the guy-by-the-stop-sign would talk so long that Ek didn't have time to cross the street into the woods, a disappointment for sure, but he acknowledged that he had picked up another sermon topic or two from his homeless friend. You never have too many of those. Sermon topics. Friends.

Whenever Rev. Ek got to the other side of Stateline Avenue he had crossed the border between Wisconsin and Illinois and was entering into where The Creek flows into Rock River. Parts of it are as woodsy and natural looking as the Upper Peninsula of Michigan.

The Visitor

As Rev. Ek stuck his head into the outer office of the church the Monday morning before the dream, Sandy met him with her usual cheery smile and said, "She's waiting for you in there, in your kingdom."

"Who?"

"You know. That girl–woman–that you talked to after church on Sunday. I heard about it. Remember, there was a queue waiting to shake your hand and tell you how wonderful you were? They acted like they were restless, but I think they liked it, your chatting her up. She is so attractive and the word is out that you held her hand a long time, like you didn't want to let it go. Did you?"

"So, she's in there right now? In my office? What's she want?"

"I don't know," Sandy said. "She acted like she might have had an appointment. Like you'd be expecting her. Were you?"

Ek didn't say anything.

"Well, aren't you going in there? You afraid of something?"

Rev. Ek's office was huge and nicely presented, but unfinished. Like him, a work in progress. At an auction that raised money for Belle Waters's symphony orchestra, Ek had bid on an item that was described as "A room embellishment by professional interior decorators. You provide the room and raw materials–furniture, etc.–and we will make it irresistible." His bid of three hundred dollars prevailed. What quickly became known as his little kingdom was taking shape.

Pictures and paintings were placed not too high or too symmetrical: a print of The Triumvirate of British golf greats from the turn of the last century, a map of the Old Course at St. Andrews, a photo of a teenaged Jesus in jeans and a rust-colored plaid shirt, an oil painting of two Canada geese nibbling near cattails, a pencil-sketch of Gandhi. A dirty looking sheepskin rug from Scotland hung on the windowless east wall next to a Mennonite quilt with patches of colorful farm fields. The north wall shelf between the windows was covered with books about religion. Rev. Ek inherited lots of them from his predecessor and stuffed in a hundred more of his own. He arranged two sofas face to face in the northwest corner with a coffee table in between. A place for serious conversation. Everyone who saw the room for the first time oohed and aahed over the bare oak floors, but Ek thought they still needed something, like a section of soft carpeting or throw rugs or a practice putting green.

The visitor had made herself at home in one of the wingback faux leather chairs. She stood up when he came in and looked him in the eye.

"Hi," he said. "You came back. You weren't kidding."

"Of course not," she said. "That sermon yesterday got to me, but do you ever allow your parishioners to quiz you afterwards? Like let them–us–be Monday morning quarterbacks?"

"Of course. Throw me a pass, but what's your name?"

"It's Jayne," she said. "Jayne Nova."

They looked at each other. Finally, he said, "I'm Pastor Christopher, or Chris."

"I know," she said. Then switching to a different sport with a nod to the clubs Pastor Ek had leaning against a file cabinet, she said, "I'm not a real golfer, but my uncle is. He's nuts about that game and has lots of golfing friends. I thought of them Sunday when you laid that big message on us. You called it the big message, right?"

"I did."

"Just how did you put it? Refresh my memory."

"Well, I said that in golf they teach you not to cheat, but in most games, they teach you not to get caught cheating. Quite a difference."

She said, "And then you gave us a homework assignment. To keep a little log about where these things might apply in our own lives. You know, like in games people play or whatever."

He looked right at Jayne Nova. A tickle scampered up and down his back. She was slim and tall for a girl–woman–compared to him, anyway. About five eight with a big, slightly bucktoothed (beautiful!) grin. A shock of untamed reddish hair tumbled down her forehead. She would brush it back several times that morning. And was she just a tiny bit cross-eyed?

Jayne said, "Well, tell me more."

He began, "I want to get people thinking about these things. Golf has become another little world for me. A place where many things seem clear-cut. They get played out right before my eyes. Plus, I need sermon topics. It provides them. Some of them. Obviously, life is more complicated than golf."

"Duh," she said as they locked eyes and smiled.

Then Ms. Nova scowled. "Okay, maybe you can help me with a couple of things. Golf, it's a game for rich people, right? Country club types like my uncle? Well, I've never heard of a community of believers whose public face is golf, but that's what it looks like this church is becoming in Belle Waters, thanks to you. I don't know if you planned it this way, but people mention golf right away when they talk about Fair Are the Meadows. This house of God, or is it a house of golf?" She expected him to smile, but he didn't.

"Look," he said. "If they are talking about this place at all, I like it. If we're getting a reputation for anything in this community, I'm for it. Remember that bit that says even bad publicity is what? Publicity! Right? I like it when people talk about churches."

"Even if it's tied to something that's negative?" she said.

"What's negative about golf?" Ek said with a prickle of attitude.

"Oh, come on. You gotta be kidding. It's a plaything of the haves."

"I've heard that complaint many times, sometimes from my friends. A few of them hate golf, or I should say they come across as thinking it's a waste of time at best and downright anti-poor people at worst. I used to think like that sometimes, but now here's how I push back: Number one: it's great exercise . . ."

Jayne Nova interrupted, "Wait a minute. You call riding around in those little cars–or carts, or whatever they call them–exercise?"

"No, no, no," Ek said. The exercise comes from walking the course and carrying your clubs. Not many people do it that way, in the United States anyway, but I do and so do most golfers in the UK and Ireland, the walking part anyway. Over there lots of them use pull carts. They call 'em trollies. A few players have caddies, but they're disappearing–the caddies–a fact that is one of my pet peeves . . ."

Jayne Nova was ready to say something. Ek held up his hands, palms toward her, ". . . but here's my second point. One reason that privileged people choose golf is because the game is so wonderful."

She appeared to spit at him. "C'mon. Get serious."

"Okay, let me put it this way," he said. "People with money can try all kinds of things. Enough of them over the decades–centuries–have found that golf has something to offer. Something good. It's like the arts. Golf is an art form."

Ms. Nova wheezed so hard that something flew out of her nose and landed on his pants leg. At first, they just looked at it, and then they laughed hard. That quaking and shaking that you can't control. Sandy stuck her head in and asked what's up. Ek shooed her away with, "We're into some finer points of theology."

As Sandy left, she thought, "*There once was a member of this congregation who wrote a book about humor in religion. A Belle Waters College professor. Byers or Meyers or something like that.*"

Ms. Nova took the opportunity to leave then too. Ek's heart raced. His palms were wet. Later when he popped into Sandy's office to get a cup of coffee, he said, "What do you know about that woman? Jayne Nova."

"Not much. She's a visiting professor at the college. I asked her what she taught and she said psychology and education. 'Stuff like that.' Then she said she's interested in games people play. She teaches a course with that title. They study what she called every conceivable example of playful pursuits. Her favorite is mind games. I said, 'Pastor Chris sure likes golf.' She said, 'No kidding.' She seems very confidant, Ms. Nova. You know who she reminds me of?"

"Who?"

"Katharine Hepburn that golden oldie actress. She looks like her and moves like her. Did you know, she was a good golfer, Miss Hepburn?"

"I didn't. I don't," Chris said. "I don't know anything about her."

"Well," Sandy said, "Golf and acting were not her only talents."

At home, later that day Rev. Ek Googled Katharine Hepburn and learned about her fierce independence and spirited personality along with her golfing accomplishments and ongoing love affair with Spencer Tracy. He wanted to watch their film *Pat & Mike* which shows off her golfing talent, but it wasn't available so he downloaded another one, *Woman of the Year*, and watched the whole thing.

Walking the Walk

During his next lesson Chris Ek told Keyshawn Gentry about the conversation with Jayne Nova. Slowly rotating back and forth in his swivel chair with his chin in his right hand and eyes right on the man of God, Gentry listened intently and then turned evangelical.

In a soft, bass voice he preached, "You see the big picture better walking. When you're on foot heading right at your ball, you get a focused look at what you gotta do. Racing around in a cart takes that away. In a cart you're usually riding with another guy, right? It seems like a nice social arrangement, but don't forget this: you ride to your partner's ball, he hits it, and then you both whip around and head for your ball. The zig zaggy route gets in the way of concentrating on what you have to do next. Okay? You see what I mean?"

"Reverend" Gentry's preaching was to a choir of one. Ek agreed with what he was hearing, but he couldn't resist being a devil's advocate. He said, "But riding in a cart together is so sociable . . ."

". . . C'mon," Gentry interrupted. "Walking does that better, and you don't have to put up with the bumps and twists and gas fumes and noise."

"Electric carts don't have fumes, and they're quiet, like Priuses."

"Okay, I'll concede that electric carts are better than gas ones, but they can't come close to the joys and benefits of walking."

"Amen to that," Rev. Ek said.

Then he told his teacher about his golfing grandparents in Florida, the hole in one, and the tightening grip golf had on him in spite of his modest skills. And he told him about one of his early confessional sermons at Fair Are the Meadows Family Church where he admitted that the hole in one frenzy in Florida caused him to get light-headed. "I looked out at the congregation and said, 'I never realized how big a deal a hole in one is to golfers. Those miracles can lead to religion, and on that day, I was converted. I became a believer in–I slowly said–GEE-OH and waited. The congregation called out EL EFF! I wagged my finger at them and softly said Nooooo. *Dee.*' Then in a burst of uncharacteristic spontaneity, I added, 'Okay, I admit, you're right. It was el eff. I wasn't thinking of God at the time.' They loved it. The congregation."

Next Ek told Gentry how he broke from the prepared text of one of his other sermons–about the excesses of individuality in society these days– and asked the congregation if any of them had ever had a hole in one. Two women raised their hands, and one of them started describing the details of how she did it. Out loud to the congregation: the way the ball bounced into the hole, what club she used, the wind direction. She could have gone on forever, but others interrupted her with questions and corny jokes. During the sermon! "*Things have gotten out of control,*" I thought, but then thought again. "*Not totally. There are epiphanies that come with holes in one, and new ways to see ourselves and our self-centeredness.*"

Back home that afternoon he scribbled a note reminding him to some-day preach a sermon on other kinds of holes-in-one. Unexpected, perhaps life-changing highs that have nothing to do with golf.

3

Troubles

A Bad Thursday

JOYCE AHLGREN TAUGHT SUNDAY school at Meadows Church. After many years she still maintained her enthusiasm for the kids and the lessons she shared. Stories actually. Some came from the Bible, some from the week's news or scuttlebutt around town, some from her own years as a child going to a Lutheran church in Rockford, some from her time in the Peace Corps in Namibia, and some she just made up.

It's not easy getting good Sunday school teachers in the first place, and the ones who stick with it year after year come from heaven. Joyce Ahlgren was an angel. Every night Rev. Ek said a little prayer of thanks for her. Early in his ministry at Meadows, he had come to the conclusion that here was an authentic Christian. In the flesh, right in front of him. A true believer who embodied love and empathy and grace and modesty and other good qualities. She was a model for adults as well as kids. That's what The Reverend Christopher Hilding Ek thought, anyway. He never shared this impression in so many words with others but he believed it, and he sensed that others at Meadows felt the same way. He thought, "*I wonder if every minister has somebody like her. I am so blessed.*"

Mrs. Ahlgren's own children had gone through her Sunday school class over the years, and the last of them, fourteen-year-old Paige, was now taking confirmation with Pastor Ek. Outwardly, he liked the girl–he liked everyone–but after one unpleasant little episode, he wrote this into his dairy: "*She's got a way to go to be like her mother. I feel sorry for Joyce Ahlgren having to put up with Paige day after day, but what do I know about adolescents? Members of the church think I understand them–the kids. Heck, I can't even analyze my own teen-age years with any confidence. But this Paige. She gets to me. Why?"*

A few days earlier Ek had been in his office discussing a Sunday school lesson with Mrs. Ahlgren. Paige had tagged along and was sighing and rolling her eyes in response to what the adults were saying. Then she spoke harshly to her mother. *"Talking back and nasty!"* Chris wrote in his journal. He was shocked to witness what he took as her attack on the Sunday school saint, but didn't say anything. Afterwards the three of them stayed quiet for what seemed like forever. Something always breaks the spell in situations like this. The daughter finally broke into tears and fell into her mother's arms.

And so Ek was impressed once more with Joyce Ahlgren. It had to do with her calmness. Her lack of ego. Her savvy as a parent. Her ability to let people feel free to emote in her presence. Her open arms. Her tolerance of silence. Her apparent unconditional love for her daughter, the person in his confirmation class whom he would sometimes think of as This Child. And eventually as This Trouble Maker. This young preacher.

If Chris had to boil his early impression of Paige down to one word it would be *confident*. She directly took on other people. She moved with certainty, and she embodied the need to physically project one's move from childhood to adulthood. A touch of eyeliner, a tiny blue streak in her long auburn hair. Jeans that were damaged just a little, and washed a lot. Pale green fingernails.

But then there are these tears. "She's just a kid," Chris thought at the time, but never again.

After Paige left the room, Joyce said four words to Pastor Ek that in hindsight signaled a turning point in his very young ministry. She said, "I'm angry . . ." followed by awkwardness where she just stared at him, and then she added ". . . at you."

Ek snapped to attention with the first two words, but stayed quiet as his face turned red. He thought she was kidding with the next two, but the look on her face said she wasn't. His right eyelid twitched and his mouth went dry. Later he would feel hurt, but in the moment, he managed to stammer, "What on earth is the matter?"

"It's that group."

"What, your Sunday school kids?"

"No, no." She made little quotation marks in the air, "What you call 'The Discussion Group'. Our meeting yesterday pushed me over the edge."

"Yeah, we are a bunch of heretics," he said with a forced laugh.

"Believe me, Pastor, what I have to say is not funny. I'm going to quit teaching Sunday school."

Ek's blood pressure spiked. He said, "Wha- what are you talking about? Please don't do that. We need you. If you retire we won't have a Sunday school program."

"I'm not retiring, I'm quitting. I've had it with the wishy-washiness of this place. This church. I apologize for these words, but I mean it. Yesterday's Discussion Group session put on the straw that broke my back."

"What are you talking about?"

"It's the things we grapple with there. They make such sense, yet on Sunday mornings we go on and on–*you* go on, you lead us–into saying things or believing things that just aren't so."

"Like what?"

"I don't want to go into it now, but Paige, she's frustrated with you, too, and she's right."

Joyce Ahlgren did go on a little bit longer. "Let me try to put it into a few hastily chosen words and then I've got to go: From the pulpit in front of your flock you don't seem to value the same things that you support in other settings, like when you are with our Discussion Group."

He just sat there looking at her.

She went on. "There are people we read who say that the words at-tributed to Jesus in the bible were in all probability not spoken by him and that none of the miracles ever happened. The Reverend Dr. Bishop John Shelby Spong–she spat out the words– is one guy you seem to like who talks like this."

Rev. Ek interrupted her. "Spong calls them metaphors or symbols or signs."

Mrs. Ahlgren said, "Yeah, and that's what drives me crazy, and I'm only slightly exaggerating. In my class of pre-teens, if I said everything is a story or symbol or metaphor, I know that the wrath of quite a few parents would follow. Remember that line from some of the forceful fundamentalists in our flock. They say our denomination is called The United Church *of Christ*. Of Christ! The wise people of our past didn't choose to say 'of Jesus.' It's of Christ. There's a difference."

"*Duh,*" he thought, but stayed quiet.

"Why can't you tell it like it is, or like you were taught at seminary? We need your leadership in reconciling things like this. Why can't you do this?"

He said, "I don't know," but thought "*Don't I do that?*"

Joyce Ahlgren got up and left, raging inside and questioning her own dedication to this church.

Understanding Golf

After his next golf lesson Christopher Ek said to Keyshawn Gentry, "You use the term 'It's in the dirt' quite a bit. Where does that come from?"

"Ben Hogan. Hogan was a great practitioner of the rule that nothing beats hitting hundreds of balls every day. We can preach swing thoughts and fundamentals all we want but what really matters is that discipline of contacting that ball with the club face square, and mother earth gets tweaked much of the time which is the way it should be as long as you hit the ball before the ground. It's a dirty business, golf." He smiled.

"So, Hogan is one of your hard-working heroes?"

"Oh, I suppose so, but I was brought up on Tiger Woods. He was—is—a living example of the value of practice. Have you heard the story of him and Earl Woods early on at the Navy golf course in Long Beach?"

"I don't think so."

"Well, Tiger wasn't even ten years old when Dad—Army Lieutenant Colonel Earl Woods—first brought him out there with the idea of playing some holes together, but they didn't get to do that. Right away, anyway. Tiger was judged to be too young, but it may have turned out to be a blessing in disguise. The little guy practiced his short game for hours while Earl and his buddies played holes. Tiger came to covet—as you ministers might say—those times around the practice green, and Earl recognized an opportunity to—I'm going to call it—incentivize the scene. The dad wouldn't let the kid go to the course to practice until he got his homework done. That's how the legend goes, anyway. It makes sense to me considering how the adult Tiger is considered one of the hardest working golfers ever in spite of his recent difficulties in tournaments and life."

"So, Tiger's your hero?"

"Well, sure. Along with some others. But Tiger's a complicated guy and I don't know if he would be one of your better Sunday school heroes, but I love it when a black guy like Tiger, or VJ Singh, or me is known for being a hard worker.

"*You* sure are," Chris said.

Ek wanted to learn more about this man he had grown to respect and like. He asked, "Who are your other golf gurus, *Professor* Gentry?"

Gentry paused and finally whispered, "The writers. It took me a while to realize that my playing ability wasn't going to help me make a living on one of the big time professional golf tours or even compete now and then at the state level, but the teaching that comes through words really got to me—gets to me."

"From who . . . whom?"

"Well, Harvey Penick and Michael Murphy top my list but Herbert Warren Wind and John Updike are there."

"Updike the novelist?"

"Oh, he loved golf. He wasn't a great player by any means, but he had insights into the game that are jewels. You should read his book *A Month of Sundays*. It's about a congregation of wayward clergy cooling off at a rehab place in the southwest. Out in the desert in Arizona or New Mexico or somewhere. They play cards and golf while serving their sentences usually for sexual or financial offenses. At one point Updike has his protagonist hitting a perfect five iron shot and proclaiming 'That's it. That's God.' I think that's how he put it. I've read that book more than once. I am hereby requiring it for you. Okay?"

They smiled at each other.

"Okay," Ek said, "Updike's going to be on my to-do list, but what about the other ones, Penick and Murphy?"

"Harvey Penick was one of the great teachers whose public writings emerged late in life–when he was in his eighties. For decades Penick worked with many of the finest women pros as well as both Tom Kite and Ben Crenshaw, those two Texas kids of the same age who turned out to have fabulous golf careers. Penick would never teach them together. He didn't want what he said to one to necessarily influence the other. They were individuals with unique ways of doing golf. Penick recognized what I think is one of the main points of teaching golf, or anything I guess: people learn differently. Teachers must build on what the students bring to the lessons. Their golfing possibilities, sure, but other things as well."

Christopher thought, *"I wonder what he thinks I'm bringing? What does my congregation think I bring now that they're getting to know me better?"* Joyce Ahlgren–former Sunday School teacher–was on his mind.

Gentry continued. "So, I also strongly suggest–No, I'm going to *require*–that you read *The Little Red Book* by Mr. Penick. That's what Kite and Crenshaw called him: *Mr. Penick*."

"What about this Michael Murphy?" Christopher asked. What do you think of him?"

Keyshawn Gentry looked Rev. Ek in the eye. "You haven't heard of Michael Murphy? You are such an innocent fellow."

Ek–sensing the playful moment–said, "Of course I am naïve about many things, oh learned teacher, but you should know that I've read *Golf in the Kingdom* more than once. Of course, I've heard of Michael Murphy. I learn something more each time I open those pages. I even brought it with me up to the pulpit during my first sermon at Meadows. Should we share our impressions of Mr. Murphy and Shivas Irons and Seamus McDuff?

"Yes. Of course. I'd love to, but not now. With all due respect, Rev. Ek, you aren't ready to get into that yet. When the time comes I'll give you my two cents' worth. By the way, do you know that Murphy's short stay in Scotland was a–how should I put it–mere prelude to a longer time in India? He spent over a year at the Sri Aurobindo Ashram in India."

"I do know. I'd love to go there some day, visit that part of the world or even stay for a while–I want to learn more about Gandhi–but we're still talking about learning golf, right? What about *Golf Digest* or "*The Golf Channel?*" I cross paths with them pretty often. They're full of lessons and swing thoughts and testimonials. They must be doing something useful, aren't they?"

Gentry thought for a moment and then said, "In short, no. Okay, I have to admit that *Golf Channel* at least gives you some visuals, but lessons in *Golf Digest* magazine are almost totally useless. Every month they throw out new swing thoughts and if the reader takes them seriously, he'll fill his head until it overflows or short-circuits or crashes or something. There's way too much coming at you. Stay away from that stuff. Please."

"But *The Little Red Book* is a bunch of words. Why is it so great?"

"It taps into the wisdom of teaching anything. Not just golf. Harvey Penick was a genius at taking what a person brings to the game, potential, and building on it. But the key to Penick isn't all the to-do tidbits; it's his big picture. When I have you doing the magic move, that's from Penick. And when he says, 'Take dead aim,' to one of his students on the tour or anyone, nothing more's needed at that point. It's so simple. So pure." Keyshawn Gentry's eyes were moist, and he stopped talking.

Finally, he said, "You gotta read Penick."

Gentry paused and the silence became awkward. When he started up again, his voice was unsteady. "Some people just don't get it–the game–but they think they do. They probably play a lot of holes and in more cases than I care to count, they talk a good game, but they don't have it in their bones. And some of these characters are super slow in learning golf etiquette."

"What do you mean?"

"They don't easily learn 'the don'ts,' like don't step on another player's putting line or don't let your shadow compete for their attention, or don't play slow. What I'm talking about here is moving from shot to shot not your swing itself. But I've gotta stop there. Mr. Penick would frown at me talking so much about 'd' words: the don'ts. I've gotta say this though: another thing a serious golfer would never do is tell a joke on the tee before his group hits. I used to be paired up with a guy who did that, and it almost drove me crazy."

"What did you say to him?"

"Nothing. I should have. I just stopped playing with him. Sometimes I don't say what I should, and I regret it."

"Me too." Rev. Ek. said. "Errors of omission. You know, those are the ones that allow us religious types to say that everyone sins, because a hundred per cent of human beings can be charged with not doing enough or not speaking up when they should. Even Jesus."

Keyshawn looked at him. "Really? Like what?"

Ek blurted, "Well, he didn't play golf," and then he regretted it. The moment wasn't right for being silly.

Keyshawn Gentry smiled but stayed serious. "You know I have my pantheon of golf characters, and I'll always sing their praises and urge my best students to read them. I really identify with that mysterious guy that Michael Murphy writes about: Shivas Irons. The shelves in his musty little flat in Scotland are full of titles that you wouldn't expect."

"Is he a real character, this Irons fellow?"

"Is Christ?"

"Well, that came out of the blue. What do you mean?"

"Is the Christ or Messiah or Lord or whatever Jesus became, real? I'll tell you about my relationship with Shivas Irons if you do the same with your 'God.'"

"*Jesus Christ,*" Ek responded with his volume cranked up.

Gentry didn't know if Ek was using the name in vain, or giving an answer to his question or what. Then in one of those wonderful little coincidences that they would retell down through the years, simultaneously they said, "It's a mystery." Christopher's thoughts zapped to a favorite minister of his who would always close Holy Communion rituals with those words.

Gentry said, "When John Updike spins that tale about the wayward minister proclaiming that God has been revealed to him via a perfect five iron shot, he's showing himself as somebody who truly understands the sweetness of golf. It's something that goes deeper than charm. It captures you–the golfer–and, well, gives you confidence and pleasure. Most dedicated golfers have a story or two that gives a peek at what this means to them."

Christopher Ek said, "What are yours? Let me in on your little secrets."

Keyshawn Gentry smiled and said, "Okay, here's one, but it's not exactly a secret and, to me, it's not little."

He described a heavenly Saturday morning on a golf course near Steel, Michigan. Keyshawn was visiting some of his relatives who had taken up golf and stuck with it in spite of racial prejudices that made it hard for the game to catch on among members of the black community. The early May day was perfect: no wind, sunny, dewy, sixty-five degrees already at 9:00 a.m. heading for seventy-five. Everyone in his foursome was off to a good start through the first three holes: No double bogies. No missed three-footers. Next came a par 4 of 410 yards heading south into the sun with a still pond guarding the green. Everything looked impressionistic and smelled grassy. Leaves were coming out. Blossoms poked through pink and white. Gentry had hit a driver on the screws and was left with a seven iron from a perfect lie. He hit one of those shots that Ben Hogan always said is the hardest of all: perfectly straight. This one never left the flag stick, did a little dance, and settled four feet from the hole.

"Playing golf never has gotten any better than that for me," Keyshawn said.

"I don't get it," Ek said. What's the big deal about that? Don't good golfers do that all the time?

Keyshawn held back any expression. He said, "Shivas Irons would have gotten it. You might someday. The deep culture of golf."

"Tell me more. Please."

"Not now. Maybe someday."

Bats in the Belfry

To put it gently, most mainline Protestant churches have less than easy success with their youth programs. The old adage about getting bats out of belfries seems to apply.

Old pastor: "You know how to get rid of the bats?"

Young pastor: "No, how?"

Old pastor: "Confirm them. They won't come back."

While there are success stories here and there, the point is this: It's very difficult to attract and keep teen-agers in the church. This certainly was the case at Fair Are the Meadows prior to Christopher Ek getting his call. During interviews, he said it would be a top priority if he were chosen: getting kids to come to church and stay.

He got unanimous support from the governing board on that one. "We'll try anything!" they said, and for a while what Pastor Ek introduced seemed to be working. The guiding principle was: expect a lot from every person and give them stimulating resources. In practice, this turned out to mean allowing lots of freedom as long as they expected a lot of themselves and dug into resources, like books.

Pastor Ek started by having them read *The Juvenilization of American Christianity* by Thomas Berger. They liked the irony of being able to criticize "juveniles" who were adults. Next, he assigned *If Nuns Ruled the World: Ten Sisters on a Mission* by Jo Piazza. Highlighting the contributions of Catholic women appealed to his ecumenical and feminist values, and he got no argument from the class. A third book flirted with the bats in the belfry dilemma. It was by Barbara Brown Taylor who described her mixed feelings about the shortcomings of organized religion in *Leaving Church: A Memoir of Faith.*

For a while they were on a roll, Pastor Ek and his kids. He wanted to propose that they consider doing book reviews via non-verbal video-taping that they could turn into YouTube creations–Publicity for his church and youthfulness for Christ–but before he could share the idea with them, Paige Ahlgren convinced the class that they should do something else: act out what she called issues that confront the church. In little one act skits. The others agreed, it moved to the head of the proposals queue, and they gave it a try.

The first attempts had mixed reviews. The kids had a good time by not taking the project too seriously, and it became a contest to see who could create clever lampoons. Adam & Eve in the Garden of Eden was performed at an organic farm east of town. Another Genesis story came from the perspective of the serpent (A local amateur herpetologist loaned them a gently constricting king snake). Sampson & Delilah did their thing first in an exercise space at the "Y" and then at a popular barber shop down town. Moses's life spun by with kids portraying him from infancy through a troubled adolescence to his white beard period.

They avoided themes from the New Testament. Pastor Ek wondered if they assumed it was off limits–You don't make fun of Christ–but he soon learned that you do make fun of Christopher Hilding Ek, whom the kids had dutifully referred to as Pastor Chris until one of them asked,

"Could we call you Chris or Christopher, without the Pastor bit or how about Christ, without the o-p-h-e-r?"

Another said, "Pastor Christ?" and the room exploded with laughter. (Paige had been calling him that behind his back.) The speaker was trying to be funny, but he didn't expect such a dramatic reaction. Without thinking, he added, "Well, this guy–he nodded toward Pastor Ek–is Christ-like, in my opinion anyway," and the room calmed down.

Then one of them said, "How about Che, like that Cuban revolutionary who was trying to change everything. Those are his initials: Christopher Hilding Ek."

Paige leaned in the direction of Ek, and shot back, "This guy's no revolutionary."

To himself, Ek agreed. Eyes down the pastor smiled, and said, "Well, let's move on." He liked that they made fun of him.

Paige had created a skit that was contemporary and direct. It had the title "Does this church–*our church*–juvenilize adults and teach them fairy tales?" The idea came to her at home where she had seen highlighted pages from Spong's book *The Fourth Gospel: Tales of a Jewish Mystic*, something her mother was reading for that discussion group. It was about human words that don't adequately address the main message: Jesus is messiah or– some would–say Lord.

"Why doesn't Pastor Christopher do that? Say it out loud to the whole congregation?" Paige had asked her mother.

"Daughter, you've been reading my mind."

Falling Asleep

As he strolled south from the post office one day, Christopher Ek didn't see his homeless friend sitting by the stop sign, so he was free to cross Stateline Avenue right away, wade through The Creek, and disappear southward into those woods along the east bank of the Rock River. Ten minutes beyond where the free-flowing tributary emptied into the river, he reached into a cache of fishing paraphernalia he had hidden away and threw a line into calm backwaters. He didn't care if he caught anything or even had a nibble. He lay on his back, rested his head against a log, and drifted into that sweet state when you're falling asleep and know it. Rev. Ek needed the solitude and quiet. Soon he was dead to the world around him.

He was a caddy standing on the first tee inhaling the smell of newly mown grass, eager to set off. It was early May: windless, sunny, dewy, sixty-five degrees by early morning and heading for seventy-five. The anticipation of caddying energized him: The stretching and lifting. The sights and sounds. The walking. Therapy for body and mind.

Ek didn't care a hoot about his golfer's–his "bag's"–ability, but when he saw her take a practice swing, he could hardly keep from laughing out loud (It emerged as a stifled snort). She held the club cross-handed and made a little run at an imaginary ball before swinging at it like a hockey player. She almost fell over when her weight shifted on the follow-through. She wound up with her shoulders perpendicular to her intended line of flight. Happy Gilmore Goofy.

This person–this "golfer"–had acknowledged her shortcomings when they first met. "Tell me what I'm doing wrong," she said, "and keep a careful count on how many shots I take." She seemed to crack a smile, or was it a sneer?

Business-like now she addressed the ball for her first drive of the day, and whiffed it. In a flash, she dug into her pocket and threw down a second ball, rather than taking another swipe at the one still on the tee. "Odd," Ek thought, "but she is one of God's precious individuals, and I must be patient." Her second swing produced a perfect drive. The ball soared like it was climbing a ski-jump. A big hit with hang time.

From what Ek could tell, the two of them were the only ones on the course as they marched down the first hole, he a half-step behind. She fanned her next shot, whipped another ball out of her pocket, and put it on a tee even though they were in the fairway. Addressing the dimpled sphere with her furrowed brows and stiff arms, she wiggled and waggled and shuffled around for ten seconds–an eternity–doing what golfers normally call a pre-shot routine.

At this point Ek stopped her and said, "Ma'am, you asked me to tell you what you're doing wrong. Here goes. You need to grip the club with your left hand above your right. Take dead aim. Choose a target and stick to it. Stand still when you swing. Pull the club back slowly, and keep your eye on the back of the ball at all times. Make a full shoulder turn. Start your downswing with your left foot planting into the ground. Use a tee only for your first shot on a hole. You've gotta follow the rules. Relax and think of no more than one thing as you're trying to hit the ball. Amen. That's it, for now."

During this sermonette, the golfer stood legs apart, hands on hips, with a gray, evil look. When Chris stopped talking she said,

"So, are you finished?"

"Yes, ma'am."

"Well, then you can go straight to hell, and stay there. You're fired." And she got ready to attempt the next shot on her own terms.

He stood stock-still.

She hit a superb shot from the teed "lie," picked up her bag of clubs, threw it over her shoulder and headed toward the green never looking back. As he watched her climb toward the green, from off in the distance somebody yelled FORE and he jumped . . .

"What are you here . . . FORE!?"

. . . the voice said, and Ek snapped awake. In measured enunciation, a scruffy looking guy added, "In case you haven't figured it out, you're trespassing." The pastor shielded his eyes from new light as spittle ran out the right side of his mouth. "But, hey, relax," the guy said. "I'm not going to hurt you. What are you doing here?"

"Fishing. I fell asleep."

In a very soft voice the guy slowly said, "You should know this is a special place. I'm one of the caretakers. My friends and I try to monitor what goes on–who comes and goes. I've seen you before."

Ek didn't respond.

"You're not the only one who sneaks in here. People are doing something with our land, and it's got us worried. Big shots are turning it into–oh, I don't know–an educational or historical site or something. They call it the divergence."

"Convergence," Ek said. "They call it The Convergence. It's where The Creek runs into the river back there. (He tilted his head to the north.) Indians lived there first. It has historical implications for the Stateline area."

"So, you are one of them? The people who will want to clear us out?"

"No. No, of course not," Ek said too quickly. "I'm just a–he was about to say humble little country pastor but thought again–guy who lives in Belle Waters."

"What do you do there?"

There are those times when clergy like to keep their vocational identities to themselves as they meet strangers in order to stay a part of the anonymity that can leave things relaxed and casual. To avoid the inevitable re-setting of perceptions when the truth is discovered. To keep the language candid and from the heart. This was one of those times.

Ek said, "I'm looking for something. Haven't found it yet." Immediately, he wished he hadn't added that second bit.

"Me too," the guy said. "You come here often, do you?"

"When I can. It's so peaceful."

"May I be frank with you?" the guy said.

"Of course."

"When you and your type barge in here, it's no longer peaceful for me and my brothers. We see you, even though you don't see us. You come in here like you own the place, picking up stuff that must look like junk, but it's ours. Fishing gear. Old blankets. You guys coming here is what Native Peoples experienced with the river of Europeans barging west. An unstoppable flood."

Rev. Ek didn't know what to say out loud, but he realized that this man must know The Guy-by-the-Stop-Sign and probably that guy out at the golf course the other day? Nervous, Ek asked what must have come across as a silly *non-sequitur*: "Do you play golf?"

"Not much anymore, but I still design a few holes here and there."

"You are a–what do they call them–golf course architect?" Ek's voice was high and weak.

"You might say so, an amateur one."

Ek focused. "Please, tell me more."

This apparently homeless man described how he got exposed to golf at a course near Chicago that was ahead of its time. It eagerly welcomed people of all colors–including him–to play and caddy. He started out by toting bags and then golfed on Mondays when caddies could play free. From the start, he was aware of the artistry of golf holes. The natural raw material that made them challenging and pleasing to the eye. To him, golf holes were sculptures to move through as a player or to develop and tweak as an architect if they didn't live up to their potential. He noticed some of these on the course where he caddied and suggested changes to the owners of the place. They listened and followed his advice.

This guy-at-the-confluence told Chris how he had joined the United States Army and lost contact with golf. When his enlistment was up he tried to get jobs in various places without success. He failed at finding a home too. From a cousin, he heard about this place where the creek runs into the river. In desperation, he moved here a year ago.

Ek said, "Do you still design golf holes?"

"I'm working on one now. Wanna see it?"

"Sure."

They walked downstream through a muddy stretch, fighting thick underbrush before breaking through to a vista that gave Ek goose bumps.

"It's not quite ready, but maybe you can see what I have in mind."

They were looking at what reminded Chris of the twelfth hole at Augusta National Golf Club in Georgia, host of the Masters' Championship: a shallow-greened par three with water in front and trouble in back. A diabolically fair test for the pros that gets his juices flowing every April when it's on television. It's the hole that destroyed Jordan Spieth back in 2016.

Ek's head was spinning. He coughed out, "Wow. What a hole." They stood there silently, and then he said, "Hey, I'm sorry, I gotta go."

"Hey, no problem," the guy-by-the confluence said.

After an awkward handshake, the pastor headed north to another world.

4

Clergy Need Help

Liturgists

By EACH WEDNESDAY THE marquee in front of Fair Are the Meadows Church called out the title of the next Sunday's sermon, like *Caretaking in the Garden of Eden* with readings from Genesis. Traditionally at Meadows, readers of scriptural passages–the liturgists–would be recruited from the congregation in advance of Sunday services when they would proceed to the front of the sanctuary along with the minister.

Pastor Ek introduced another way.

Without having any liturgist lined up in advance or without any public notice of the change, one Sunday he said from the pulpit: "Become my scriptural partner. Join me up here in reciting holy words. Right now. Please come forward." This heartfelt plea was met with silence, downcast eyes, and stone still bodies. He finally looked at Daphne Hobson, and she graciously cooperated.

After a couple of Sundays there were plenty of ready volunteers, and everyone appreciated the spontaneity, freshness, and surprise that came from not knowing who was going to read until the moment when some eager beaver rushed to join the pastor up front. A fringe benefit of the new practice for Ek was a better-informed membership. More people than ever read biblical passages in advance just in case they got the urge or felt the pressure to give it a try.

On the Garden of Eden Sunday, Jayne Nova popped up and marched briskly to the front in response to Pastor Ek's invitation. She beat out several less assertive types who had been practicing pertinent passages during the week, but weren't quick enough out of the pews when the moment came.

Ms. Nova projected herself in a lusty voice. Clear and loud. Somebody was heard saying, "She should do this every Sunday."

Pastor Ek launched into his sermon by introducing what he called a split personality from the Hebrew Bible: Adam I and Adam II. He credited *New York Times* writer David Brooks for introducing him to these characterizations in his book *The Road to Character*. Brooks says that one portrayal of Adam in Genesis can be interpreted as presenting our first man as a self-centered individual. This guy whom Brooks calls "Adam I"–and many people forever after–have behaved like they are developing material for a resume: career oriented, ambitious, and externally focused. Another side of Genesis's lead actor, whom Brooks calls "Adam II," embodies moral qualities that lead to being good and doing good. To sacrifice for others. To honor all people. To think and act beyond the moment. Words to describe particular Adam II types are often found in eulogies and obituaries.

Rev. Ek picked up on this to tell of a funeral service where he officiated earlier in the week. His homily and remembrances of the deceased wonderfully captured the essence of the person, but afterwards somebody told Ek that it's too bad that she–the dead woman–didn't hear it.

"Well maybe she did," Ek said, but thought, "*I know how we can make something like that happen at Meadows.*"

So, in the Garden of Eden sermon Ek described a practice that he had encountered at seminary: writing and publicly sharing eulogies before a person dies. To make it work the comments must be candid. This means that everything won't be all flowery and good, and it has to be orchestrated in a planned and dignified manner with some input from the–he paused–honoree. He said, "This would mean a memorial service for people like you. You who are still vertical." They smiled back.

He closed by asking, "What do you think? Could this work here?" As hands flew up and comments began, he quickly stopped them: "Let's talk after the service. Over coffee. Or when you shake my hand at the back of the sanctuary."

One person whose hand he had hoped to shake that morning was Keyshawn Gentry who had come in after the introit and sat in the back pew near the window side aisle, but Gentry must have made a quick getaway because he was nowhere to be found afterwards.

Obituaries

Eulogies for vertical people came to pass at Fair Are the Meadows. The first Living Memorial Service was for one Elizabeth "Pete" Peterson. Honoring her was proposed by members of her weekly golfing foursome, who all went to Meadows. After a little aw shucks resistance, Pete said, "Why not?" So, they and she, with tactical guidance from Pastor Ek, planned a service and spread the word so a lot of people would come.

Pete pretty much had control over the music, electronically produced in high fidelity. She chose the Swedish hymn *Children of the Heavenly Father* performed in its native tongue by the Gustavus Adolphus College choir; *Now Thank We All Our God,* played by organist Roger Nyquist; and *Abba Dabba Honeymoon,* sung by a very young Debby Reynolds. Part of a written statement in the bulletin read as follows in purposeful past tense:

"Elizabeth 'Pete' Peterson. She bent her left arm a lot on the backswing, but her golf guru said that was okay. (It was natural, for her.) She was one of the women who spoke up–bragged–about her own hole in one during the sermon when Rev. Ek shared his dramatic introduction to golf: We bring you Pete Peterson."

For the big memorial day, the other members of Pete's foursome gathered flora found on golf courses and placed them around the sanctuary: dandelions, heather, pine straw and magnolias along with a sprig of poison ivy. Bark from a tree that Pete's ball occasionally hit came with the caption "I hope Ms. Peterson felt my pain."

Mildred "Mimi" Berg gave a homily that was more roast than toast. It critiqued Pete's significantly bent arm at the top of her back swing, her [allegedly] accident producing driving of both golf balls and automobiles, and her overly rapid walking. When golfing, everyone in this foursome walked. No motorized carts. Three pulled trollies, but Pete *carried* a full complement of fourteen clubs, a fact that she wouldn't let anyone forget. The others had up to this point never revealed that they thought Pete projected a holier-than-thou attitude about her toned body and how it got that way. ("I carry my clubs!" She would say with head held high. Too high.)

But now they did. This living memorial service gave them an opportunity to, well, tell the truth. They piled on Pete in a burst of unrestrained candor: In unison they taunted, "Na-na-na, na, naaaaa . . . you think you are so smart and physically fit and with it. The next time you strut ahead of us like you own the place we might just aim our shots at your big butt." Pete's butt wasn't that big, but she did get the message. It was sobering and upsetting to learn how her friends reacted to a habit that she thought was virtuous.

But other emotions carried the day when she heard them say:

"You are the most loyal, generous friend I could ever have."

"You never gossip about anyone."

"You give, give, give," and then after a pause, "but you have never conceded anyone a putt."

"You really get golf. You know the rules without being a fanatic. You teach youngsters to play right, and in an uncanny way, you get them to treasure traditions of golf while playing golf. Not everyone understands what that means."

And then a comment from Mimi that made Pete tear up and smile at the same time: "You are a member of my fantasy life-time foursome."

Pete fired back, "What about your after-life foursome, the one for all eternity. Who's in that?"

Not missing a beat Mimi said, "Annika Sorenstam, Moe Norman, [she paused for what seemed like an eternity] and of course, you."

The "mourners"–what else could you call them?–broke into applause, and Pastor Ek signaled the kid in charge of the sound system to bring things to a close with *"I'll be loving you, always,"* by Doris Day.

The Teacher from Steel

Keyshawn Gentry was attentive when Pastor Ek started talking about church rather than golf at the start of what was supposed to be a lesson on the basics of a fluid swing. Ek said, "I saw you at Meadows a couple of Sundays ago, sitting in that back pew along the windows. I was hoping we could talk afterwards."

"Oh, I didn't recognize anybody I knew, so I made a quick exit. Sorry."

"Hey, no problem. I didn't know you were a church-going guy. I hope I wasn't pressuring you into . . ."

". . . Oh, no, no, no," Gentry said. "I was a church guy in Steel . . . Michigan. Me and my family's backsides polished the fourth row of pews until a year or so after confirmation when I (ahem) took a leave of absence. I haven't been a faithful member as an adult either, but my heart needs that stuff. Once in a while anyway. I don't get my religion solely from Michael Murphy and Shivas Irons."

Ek smiled.

Gentry continued, "I was fascinated by your living obituary idea and regret that I missed the one for Pete. Did you know she's one of my students? Golfers are easy to talk about at memorials. Their physical selves are so vivid."

"What do you mean?" Ek said.

"Well, we're sculptures in motion out there on the course. Three dimensions of space, plus one of time. Our playing buddies can't help but know our bodies from every angle. In town, I sometimes recognize golfers from way off by the way they walk. Of course, you're one of them, Pastor Ek, when you swing the clubs, but also when you move around in the front of church. Your body does things that have become a part of your swing . . ."

". . . like what?" Ek was all ears.

"Well, the way you grip the sides of the pulpit when you're getting all fired up is like how you grab onto a club. Your knuckles turn white. By the way, we need to work on getting your palms more opposed, and you're too tense. And when you wander around up there, you shuffle. Not good. Lift those feet. It helps your leg muscles and you won't look like an old man. You won't get your spikes caught in the grass. [Ek flashed back to the scene from his going-down-the-aisle dream] But your message of life being so short and time moving so fast–your sermon–is what got me thinking. We've got to turn your swing into a thing of beauty before it's too late. How old are you?"

Ek hacked out a laugh. "Well, twenty-seven, but can't golf be played for decades, and didn't John Updike say that it's the only sport where you can truly still be improving into your sixties?"

"Yeah, I guess so, but if you can groove a swing early–get the fundamentals hard-wired into your body–it'll stick with you. Extreme examples of this are found in the great ones: Bobby Jones, Sam Snead, Mickey Wright, Jack Nicklaus and Tom Watson who came within one stroke of winning the British Open at age 59. Those legends are so fortunate. It's as if they were born with it–the pure swings."

"Shouldn't you include Tiger?"

"I don't think so. He's fighting to bring back his natural moves. Time will tell if he ever gets them, but I'd be surprised. He's had too many teachers telling him all kinds of different things. He needs to trust himself when it counts–easy for me to say and hard for him, or anyone, to do–and he's too bulked up. Golfers need suppleness, not Popeye muscles. And of course, he's had all those operations. A tough task coming back. I suppose we should never sell him short." But can he trust his swing these days, like before?"

Ek thought, "*I don't trust myself when it counts, in golf or in church.*"

Gentry continued, "A great swing can be built. Ben Hogan is the prime example. For years he was good, but when he discovered what he called his secret, he became the greatest striker of the ball ever. He never was a super putter though, like Nicklaus and Woods in their primes."

Keyshawn Gentry stopped. He had finished his little sermon, but Ek wanted more.

He said, "Were you a natural in golf?"

Gentry laughed, "Good god, no, but I think I know a little bit about how to develop it in others with the help of my pal Harvey Penick and those literary characters from Scotland, along with a Canadian called Moe."

"You've probably told me this before," Ek said, "but what made Penick so successful? Did he have a secret, like Hogan?"

"It's no secret, but all golf teachers should memorize what he did: take people from where they are and build on it. This may not sound like the way to unlocking a natural swing, but Penick and Shiva Irons and me–I–believe that if golf can dissolve into our souls, we'll have a sweet future, the ball hitting part and more. The point is to help learners and teachers appreciate their natural tendencies and go from there."

Ek was thinking about Paige Ahlgren. *"Could she ever build on what she has and get to be like her mother?"* He said, "Well, pardon me for getting personal, but how do these things work with you, I mean in your own life? Beyond golf? Oh, I'm sorry. You don't have to answer."

Gentry thought for a while and quietly said, "God–Whoops, I mean golf–saved my life, or is saving it. It probably can't be saved once and for all, can it? A life?"

Pastor Ek shrugged and thought, *"I don't care if I save Paige and the others, but I sure would like to get through to them."* Then he let down his guard and said, "I am having trouble with the youth of my church. I don't think they respect me." He went on to tell his golfing mentor what was bothering him: about his early successful efforts with teenagers in Chicago, but not feeling the same positive response in Belle Waters. His–he called it–losing Joyce Ahlgren as a Sunday school teacher and her sharp words toward him. His difficulties leading the governing body at Meadows. Confronting what the church should do about the homeless.

Outside of his circle of seminarian pals Pastor Ek had never shared these agonies with anyone before. It felt like a confession. Gentry waited and broke the silence with, "What are you going to do? Do you have a plan?"

Ek said, "I can tell you candidly, no."

They just sat there, heads bowed. Gentry finally said. "You've got some big-time challenges, my friend. I suppose all pastors do these days. Please forgive me for the boldness in what I'm about to say. I know how you can solve one of your problems. The youth one."

Ek looked up.

Gentry said, "Caddying. It won't take care of everything, but I know it will make your life better with young people, and they may stay in church."

Gentry then told Ek the story of how an idea took root and grew in Steel, Michigan. It started with a group of black adult golfers who linked up with kids from his church. The kids caddied for them. They didn't have to, but the project was presented in a way that made caddying and its fringe benefits very appealing: food, pay, exercise–not a popular feature at the beginning, but they hauled the clubs around and built up their hands, and calves, and shoulders. And eventually saw the benefits. And they were employed! What happened next is that most of the kids took to golf and introduced it to their own families. The game's allure spread to the church membership and some allegedly heathen golfers started attending church.

"I call it a win, win, win, or whatever. That's my summary of the key points anyway. But here is a point that I find so interesting. This whole thing had roots in Belle Waters, Wisconsin."

"How so?" Ek asked.

"Well, a guy in Belle Waters, Martin Strong, and some of his pals sponsor a golfing event every year that brings together African-American golfers from around the country. It happens in August. They compete and bond and renew acquaintances over at Muni Golf Course. Of course, they tell and retell stories. Funny stuff, but also successes, failures, new ideas. A few years ago, Steel golfers learned that Belle Waters African-Americans had a program called 'Golfing Pals.' It had led to a higher golf profile in town and helped Belle Waters and Rockford, Illinois, co-host two Tiger Woods Foundation Clinics in the early 2000s. They were the only communities in the country to twice be given this honor that served as a big boost to the Belle Waters Junior Golf Association, a program that acquaints low-income kids to golf. The Steel guys told the Belle Waters story back home. The fuse to ignite congregational caddying was lit."

Ek hadn't yet heard of the Belle Waters Junior Golf Association. And now "congregational caddying?"

Years later when the Rev. Dr. Christopher Ek was asked to speak at Keyshawn Gentry's memorial service he talked about caddying, that one word answer he got to an important question that day way back in Belle Waters.

Lincoln

Chris couldn't sleep. He tossed and turned and eventually dreamed. The scene was a Monday night meeting of the governing board of Fair are the Meadows. Uncharacteristically, he was truly in charge, leading with authority and force but he got out-voted–he was the only one in favor–of what one of them called "your zany, risky idea." Pastor Ek's response was to turn to American history. He thought,

My friends, remember that story of President Lincoln meeting with his cabinet about an important matter when they all voted against him? Lincoln summarized the situation as follows: ayes: one, nays twelve. Then he said the ayes have it. This evening you can just call me Abe, because I am going to declare my side victorious.

Chris awoke all twitchy and tense. In the dream, he wanted the board to agree to a plan that would have young people of the church caddying for them free of charge in a gesture of building bridges across generations. The members' voices in his head had babbled all at once speaking unanimously against what "President Ek" proposed:

"We can't require them to do that?"

"I ride a cart. I don't want a caddy!"

"What about other golfers in our congregation? They'll think we're taking advantage of our offices?"

"Our schedules won't match with the kids."

"What about liability?"

"They don't need to relate to our generation."

"Caddies are extinct creatures. I never see them anywhere."

"Quite frankly, Chris–Pastor Ek–that's the dumbest idea I have ever heard."

Somebody else added, *"Hear, hear, hear: I agree. Let's vote."*

They did, leading to Pastor Ek's dreamy Lincolnesque response declaring his victory. Contrary to Ek's real life experience with them to date, in the dream the governing board had eventually humbly acknowledged defeat and agreed to endorse the letter and spirit of the caddying proposal. Ek didn't remember this detail immediately upon waking, but he felt better when he finally did.

Named after Christ

The confirmation class developed the habit of talking more about their pastor's name–Christopher Hilding Ek–out of his presence. Wise cracks. Like in, "Ek is as short as a last name can get. Add Chris to it and you have a candidate for the quickest a name can be pronounced. *Kris eck.*"

"*Christ*opher" sounds religious. "Is he the second coming of Jesus?"

"'Hilding' is just plain weird."

Today one of the kids, Pauline, got everyone's attention when she looked the minister in the eye and asked with a straight face "Were you named after Christ?"

Some of them giggled. Pastor Ek smiled and said, "Probably so, indirectly. You know, Christopher or Christina or Chris or Tina are names rooted in Christianity, but they have become popular in our culture. Once I asked my parents what they had in mind when they named me, and they said they 'didn't mind' that Christopher pointed toward their religion. Kind of a lame response, I guess."

Beverly said that her grandfather's middle name was Franklin and that since he was born during the FDR administration it must have had something to do with favoring the Democrats, but her family claimed that they were all Republicans and really named Grandpa from the family tree. "Could that be possible?" she said. "I think they were closet-Democrats. I dreamed about them last night."

Gloria said, "I had a dream last night too. I was golfing like a pro. Really good. Everything I tried worked magically. I don't even play golf, but my mom does and she said I should take it up. Do you ever dream, Pastor Ek?"

"Sure," he said, and paused like he was going to say more. "*Should I tell them about my Lincoln dream? I don't know, that's getting awfully personal. That dream knew me! Do I want these kids to . . .?*"

He took the plunge and told them everything he could remember about the dream along with some background and analysis. He told them about his passion for golf and his hole in one. About his lessons from Mr. Gentry and that the two of them think golfers should walk. About the memorial service for Mrs. Peterson–Pete–that none of the kids attended.

He hadn't told about his pre-occupation with his failure in reaching the very group to whom he was speaking–them–when Paige said, "Why were we in it? Why do you think you had us caddying?"

"Good question," Pastor Ek said. "I have wondered about that too." Then in a risky move, he said, "I need you. You all. I think my dream was trying to tell me that."

"How do you need us?" Bruce asked.

Ek said, "I'm not succeeding with you. We should be like, well, like a fluid golf swing with all of its parts working together, but instead I'm . . .

". . . Whiffing? Shanking? Four-putting?" Paige rat-a-tatted with a mock attitude.

"Yeah. I need a lesson," Chris replied.

Normally, the kids would have made fun of this latest example of what they thought was his over-preoccupation with golf, but they stayed quiet, and he began to tell them about his experiences on the South side of Chicago and his frustrations about not being able to duplicate it in Belle Waters.

Finally, Paige said, "I like your dream. Let's do it."

Everyone looked at her.

"Let's get into caddying, but let's make the leaders of this church–the board–caddy for us."

"But we aren't golfers," Gloria said. "Except for a couple of us and me in my dreams."

A light bulb turned on in Ek's head. *"I'll bet Gentry could help. He has a wonderful ability of quickly getting to the heart of what it takes to hit the ball."* He said, "Let me work on that one. Thanks, Paige, and you others."

Then he turned to the scriptural focus of that day:

Second Cor 5:18-19. "All this is from God, who through Christ reconciled us to himself and gave us the ministry of reconciliation; that is, in Christ, God was reconciling the world to himself, not counting their trespasses against them, and entrusting to us the message of reconciliation."

They listened.

Taking it to the Governing Board

Pastor Ek invited members of his class to the meeting with church officers where he was determined to assertively present the caddy plan. He asked everyone to introduce themselves. Paige just happened to be last, and before she yielded the floor back to Pastor Ek *she* outlined details of the plan and at one point said things that Ek would have preferred to keep to himself. Like, "Pastor Ek says he's not succeeding with us." Pastor's blood pressure rose.

But Paige did a stellar job of presenting a rationale for the caddying idea while listing things that had to get done before it could begin, like being sure that the players know at least something about how to approach the ball and how to behave on the course. The board voted unanimously to proceed, and thanked Paige for the presentation.

In a squeaky voice, Pastor Ek said he had the answer to the next step: "I'll talk to a golf teacher, I know."

Paige said, "I'll go with you."

5

Doing God's (Golf's?) Work

Student Teachers and Caddies

GOLFING GURU GENTRY TOOK to the idea of teaching golf to Fair are the Meadows youngsters on one condition: He would be assisted by some of his young pupils who had gotten hooked on the game via the Belle Waters Junior Golf Association (aka, the BWJGA), a group with key leadership coming from African-American Belle Waterers who love golf.

"Kids teaching kids, yes! I like that idea." Gentry said, thinking "*Black kids teaching golf to white kids! Yesssss!*"

When Gentry introduces any of his young pupils to the golf swing, he focuses on time-tested fundamentals: Feet and hips square to the intended line of flight. Hands opposed in a neutral position. Same plane back and down (like Wisconsin's Steve Stricker). And then he adds, "Swing hard. Go at it."

When people–almost always adults–wonder if the hard-swinging advice works against hitting the ball squarely, Gentry points to what golf teaching professional Jack Grout told his precocious pupil, Jack Nicklaus, and Jack's parents in the early 1950's: You can best learn to groove power–a fast and effective swing speed moving into the ball–when you're young. It becomes more difficult later on.

Then Gentry tells them to watch the pros on TV. If they're laying up on a par five rather than trying to reach the green in two, they'll more than likely choose a distance that requires a full third shot. On any hole if they're hitting something short of a driver off the tee for accuracy, they still take a full swing. When parents or kids say that they just want to learn golf, not prepare for the tour, Gentry tells them "The likelihood of developing a solid swing–learning the fundamentals and pouring on the swing speed–diminishes with age. Let's capture the moment when they're still kids! And let's have high expectations. We want kids who play golf forever. Right? I sure do."

The BWJGA kids that Gentry already taught had been exposed to solid fundamentals of golf. They were polite, aware of the rules, and willing to devour the game in any weather. Into their heads Gentry had hard-wired that old Scottish axiom: Nae wind, nae rain, nae golf, meaning be prepared for anything. If during competition you are ready and your golfing adversaries are not, you have an advantage.

For starters seven BWJGA kids got together with seven from Meadows. The day was wet, windy, and cold. The first lesson had Gentry's "student teachers" instructing the Meadows kids on how to keep their hands and club grips dry via a towel draped over the sheltered underside ribs of an open umbrella and how to effectively speed up their play when the rain is coming down. In short, how to turn on "ready golf." The Meadows kids would have gotten the Scottish message eventually, but since the weather on that day was so dicey and the BWJGA kids didn't want to cancel, it turned out to showcase another benefit: when the weather is bad, fair weather folks don't come out to play. The course won't be crowded. Capture that day!

The second lesson emphasized swinging hard. The BWJGA kids had their Meadows counterparts taking assertive full swings, but without golf balls: "Any way you want to do it. Don't think of anything except swinging all out." The Meadows kids were being encouraged to be assertive.

The third and last lesson that day had everyone standing around the practice green each with three balls, but no clubs. "Roll them to the holes with your hands," the BWJGA student teachers said. "Try to get them as close as possible. Be aware how these 'putts' may curve–we golfers say 'break'–but mainly work on the distance. The kids soon realized how naturally easy it was to get the balls close that way. From under an umbrella held by Ek, Gentry was videotaping how smoothly they rolled the balls. He would keep it for a future lesson to get them chipping and pitching naturally with tools of the trade: golf clubs.

Paige Ahlgren took it all in. She would look back on this day as when she began what became an unrequited love affair with golf. She soon developed great respect for her pro Mr. Gentry, and thought of him as a wise man. In the days and years to come she would ask him countless questions about golf and life. He responded patiently and wasn't afraid to say, "I don't know." He didn't have the heart to say that she was almost hopeless as a golfer-in-the-making.

At the conclusion of the lesson on that rainy day, Pastor Ek said, "It sure looks to me like things are going well."

Teacher Gentry gave a big thumbs up and said, "We need a couple more lessons before turning them loose with the elders of your church. Next time I want my kids to caddy for yours."

Usually, Ek was deferential to Gentry, going along with whatever he pronounced about golf, but this time the minister said, "Let's do it this way: Start out with your kids caddying for mine, but on the second hole have the caddies become the players, and vice versa, and let's switch back and forth each hole. Do you see why?"

"Of course," Gentry said with a hint of embarrassment. "Why didn't I think of that, and while I am thinking, I want to get your church board out here so we can train them as caddies. Can you arrange it?"

"Yep."

Gentry was business-like when he began caddy orientation for the adults. They gathered around him at the practice green as he demonstrated the finer points of tending a flag stick: how to avoid stepping on players' intended lines, how to keep your shadow from interfering when someone is putting, and how to avoid gouging the rim of the cup when you put the flag stick back. Next, he led them to a sand trap and showed how to rake it while reminding them of the rule that golfers must not touch the sand with their club until they hit the ball. He showed them where a caddy should stand when a player is ready to hit. How to replace divots in the fairway and pitch marks on the green. And how to best carry a golf bag or pull a trolley.

Then he led them to a spot under a big maple.

Curly

Keyshawn Gentry addressed these mature folks with a mellow, sentimental tone. He began, "I was a caddy myself long ago. It was life changing. Hooked me on the game forever, but more important than that, it introduced me to people and situations that I may never have encountered. I could write a book about my bag-toting days, and I can talk endlessly about it, but please let me tell one little story now. Okay?" The church elders had planted them-selves–their bottoms–in the grass under the tree and gave Mr. Gentry their complete attention.

"When I was, oh, about eleven I first heard about caddying from some of my older sister's friends in Steel, Michigan, that town with bad water that takes so much flack these days. Hey, I still love the place. They said you could make good money at the country club, and they hire black kids. I was too young to get work there, but I was fascinated by the sight and smell of the course and would ride my bike over there just to look at it. Lush and green and hilly. Well maintained. I had never seen grass so short and thick as on those putting surfaces, and the tee boxes were about the same. Exquisite. I found a few balls and would sneak out to roll them on the greens when nobody was around, kinda like what we did with the Meadows kids the other day.

"Well, one time I was doing this putting without a putter, having a great time way out at the far end of the course with nobody around, and I lost track of time and place. A golfer–playing alone with a pull cart approached the green without my noticing it, snuck up back of me and yelled Boo! I must have jumped a foot. For a brief moment I was terrified, but then I saw his smiling face and we stood just looking at each other. He said, 'I like your putting style. You could teach me a thing or two. I've three-putted the last two holes.'

"I took him literally, and without missing a beat, asked him to hit a few putts for me to observe. He cooperated wonderfully, and I said, 'You're looking up too soon. Keep your head down until well after the ball leaves the putter. He did and sank three twelve footers in a row. He smiled after the first one, chuckled after the second one, and we both laughed out loud after the third, with thumbs up.

"Then in a mock posture of a contemplative sage fondling his goatee, he said, 'I wonder, young fella–turns out he would call me fella for years–if I could hire you to caddy for me the rest of the round.'

"I'm not old enough," I said.

"'Well, I'm the president of this club,' he said, 'and I think the membership would understand if I bent the rules a little bit. How about it?'

"I pulled his trolley for the remaining four holes. I didn't know what to say when he gave me ten dollars as we finished, but in all objectivity, I probably earned it. He one-putted three of the four greens, while following my advice on two slippery left-to-right down hillers.

"But before we parted he became embarrassed–I could see his face getting red–as he asked me my name. He said, 'I should have introduced myself and gotten to know who you are when we first met. I'm sorry. My name is Frank Williams, but everyone calls me Curly.'

"I can't remember what I said at the time, but I called him Mr. Curly for years. And I became his caddy. One of them. His favorite one. Countless times in the months and years to follow he would ask for me at the caddy shack or call my home and then drive out and pick me up. He was a very good golfer–scratch–do you know what that means?"

Blank faces looked back at Teacher Gentry until Rev. Ek piped up, "It means that you shoot about par over the long haul. It's a zero handicap. Any handicap in single digits–four or seven or nine or whatever–is pretty good, but scratch is very good. But it's possible to be even better than scratch . . ."

He stopped. Gentry had looked at Ek as if to say "Thanks, friend, you are correct, but I'm in the middle of my story. May I continue?'"

Ek stopped and Gentry continued. "Mr. Curly was a fine human being. I came to idolize him, and I know he liked me. He respected me, and treated me like an adult. As an equal. I think I can accurately say that early on I understood and practiced the culture of golf pretty well for a pre-teen. Working with Mr. Curly helped me pick up some finer points that are not necessarily obvious. Like when to speak up and when to stay quiet as a caddy. This was–is–an important communications challenge.

"Mr. Curly knew so much about golf and played so well that I first wondered what I could ever teach him, but the more times we traipsed around the course, the more I realized that he didn't know everything, and that I would occasionally notice something that could help him. For example, he had very good distance control for an amateur, but he was so fixated at getting pin high with his shots to the green that he didn't realize that being a bit short or long on a particular hole might leave him an easier putt or might allow him to err to a more forgiving spot if he didn't hit the shot perfectly. The first time I gingerly pointed this out to him, he didn't say anything, but he followed my advice and benefitted from it. It was a shot that looked like it had gone too far, but it left him with a relatively easy uphill putt, not what you would expect when you're long, since most greens slope with the high side at the back. He thanked me profusely.

"Another time I gently asked how he chose from the three wedges in his bag. He was undecided while getting ready to hit a particularly challenging chip. I said, 'What shape do you want in this one?' He looked back at me expressionless. I turned my palms up as if to say, 'It's your decision, man. Picture what you want to do.' He did and hit one in there tight.

"And I'll never forget the time when he was confronting a tricky up and down when he said, 'Fella, you decide. I'm not getting a clear image.' I looked back at him while touching one of the clubs with my forefinger. He chose it and almost holed out. That began a habit of me sending little non-verbal signals to him. It was somewhere between speaking up and staying quiet. Mr. Curly's playing companions didn't realize how we were communicating in this way while being so closed-mouthed, but he spread the word around the club house and I got a reputation of being–I feel silly saying this–somewhat of a caddying phenom.

"Until I wasn't. I'll never forget that day either. The club membership was hosting a regional 'play day' that brought in golfers from various clubs throughout the Midwest. Mr. Curly was so busy being in charge that he didn't golf himself, but he wanted me to–as he put it–show those guests a quality caddy.

"'You can earn big bucks today,' he said. 'I know of a guy who I think can learn from you and he's loaded. I've put you with him. Well, I don't really know him, but I've heard of him. I'm pretty sure it will work out well. Okay?'

"Sure," I said, "but nothing else. "I didn't say much to Mr. Curly off the golf course in those days. He called me 'Polite to a fault.' I suppose if anything I was, kinda formal. I don't know, maybe too formal."

Mr. Slinger

Keyshawn Gentry continued. "I've got to tell you about this guy I caddied for that day. Please excuse my language at a couple of points. They are his words hard-wired into my memory. He was a Mr. Slinger. With his gracious smile leading the way, Curly introduced me to him, but Mr. Slinger didn't say anything or even acknowledge me, and I thought he was gruff to Curly, but that may be my imagination in hindsight. His breath smelled alcohol and other bad fumes. It was hard to be near him. I felt like I was inhaling, well, him. Vile. The one semi-civilized thing he said to me during the whole round was, 'Where's the practice area? I've never played this course.'

"I curled my forefinger to draw him along after me, and we went to a spot at the far end of the range where a perfect pyramid of white new balls greeted us. I always thought that it was the golfer's task, not the caddy's, to break into a structure like that and pull off some balls to hit, but Mr. Slinger had another idea.

"'Well, do your job, boy,' he said. 'I'm not paying you to stand around looking at me.'

"I tensed up, but finally realized that he wanted me to tee up his drives and place balls in front of him for his iron shots. I had never seen a player ask a caddy to do that, but it didn't strike me as particularly deranged at the time. His swing wasn't that bad although he never seemed satisfied and used words–aimed at himself, I assumed at the time–that are not usually repeated in polite company. We spent a long time on that range. He would use skinny dowel rods to line up his feet, and he succeeded in keeping a handkerchief from falling out of his right armpit in order to reinforce a good body turn. At one point, he turned to me and seemed about to ask my advice, but then under his breath mumbled something I couldn't understand. By the time we finished I felt I knew his swing quite well.

"Because of Mr. Slinger's fiddling around we were late to the first tee where we joined the rest of his foursome who were already teeing off. They were strangers to each other. Mr. Curly had paired them that way in order to develop new friendships.

"After their three scattered tee shots and a doggone good one from Mr. Slinger, we headed out. He was the only one using a caddy. The others rode. We lagged behind as they raced off, but we had plenty of time since Slinger, having the longest drive, would be the last one to hit a second shot toward the green.

"He sidled over next to me and said out of the corner of his mouth, 'Boy–I'm going to call you that because I can't pronounce your name–I've heard you're a flashy caddy, but no shit, I haven't seen anything yet that leads me to that conclusion, but you've got to realize that I'm from Missouri, the Show Me State. Ya get what I mean?'

"I had no idea what he was talking about.

"Then he said, 'I don't care what kind of caddy you've been, here's what you're going to do working for me today. Yuh hear me? I've got my own set of rules. I'm gonna say this just once and quick because it looks like these assholes play fast and we may not have another chance to talk privately.'

"He recited his rules:

- If we–you–lose my ball, I'll take it out of your pay. I'm not kidding, boy.

- Don't be one of those golf rules fanatics, we aren't playing on the tour. I take the occasional mulligan, no matter who I'm playing with. If they don't like it, screw 'em.

- I believe in gimme putts. If I stab at one from inside five feet and it doesn't go in the hole, score it as if it did. Did I say I want you to keep my score? (He winked at me.)

- Don't argue with me. I had one little son of a bitch caddy who acted like I was working for him rather than the other way around. Ya hear me?

- And last but not least, I'm just a guy out to enjoy golf and try to get better. Curly–or whatever that joker's name is–says you know the golf swing. Let me know if you see some way I can improve. Okay?'

"I just looked at him. Right from the start he was the most challenging player I had ever caddied for, but until the seventh hole he hadn't done anything blatantly obnoxious or libelous. Okay, he took his mulligans and gimme putts, he swore every other word, and he had a little bottle of something he would suck on. It didn't look like it registered with him when his playing companions rolled their eyes at his behavior. One of them sidled up to me and said, 'We feel for you, kid. Stay with it.'

"On the seventh hole Slinger shanked his second shot and went into a fit of anger. I was writhing inside, but kept an outward cool. Very formally I said 'Mr. Slinger, your stance is too open and you bring the club back way too much on the inside. Trying squaring up and don't be so wristy.'

"He looked at me like I had called his mother a bad name, and then switched his anger at the world to me. 'Keep quiet, you stupid little nigger,' he said, as the others gathered around, like they were ready to protect me.

"He kept railing, and I quit right there. I walked off the course, got on my bike, and went home and straight upstairs to bed where I buried my head in the pillow. I felt dizzy, like throwing up. I knew I was done as a caddy at the club. I had violated Mr. Curly's number one rule on how to behave when your player goes crazy: Keep calm, keep quiet, and don't quit. Let the player's actions speak for themselves. Don't become a part of the scene.

"I didn't go back to Curly's club for eight days. In the meantime, Mr. Slinger's behavior was the talk of the place. He had written a blistering criticism of me, calling me a quitter along with other comments that made him look like a jerk and created sympathy for me. Some club members thought I should have finished the round, but Slinger's playing companions that day defended me, and wrote a letter saying they would have done exactly what I did. They chipped in to pay my caddy fee plus a big tip. It added up to over a hundred dollars."

A Seed

"On that eighth day Mr. Curly came to my house. He had telephoned first, and my parents told him I was in. He always treated my mom and dad so respectfully. He asked if he could talk to me alone, and they said yes.

"I was in my room reading a book by the famous explorer Roy Chapman Andrews, when Mr. Curly knocked on my door and opened it a crack. I burst into tears when I saw him. Uncontrollable soul-wrenching weeping. He moved next to me and rubbed my shoulders. Finally, he said, 'I've got something for you here,' and handed me a gorgeous wooden-shafted sand iron. "It's from the early 1930s," he said. "Back then wooden shafts were going out and big-flanged sand wedges were coming in." He said, 'I've always liked this little artifact from a juncture in golfing history.' He used those exact words.

"That gift to me was the perfect gesture by Mr. Curly," Keyshawn Gentry said to the members of the church board spread out on the grass under the maple tree. (It turned out to be the seed club in Gentry's collection of antique golf clubs that grew to hundreds over the decades.)

"We didn't talk at all about Mr. Slinger or my early departure on that day when Mr. Curly came to my room, but as he was about to leave he said, 'The members of the club and the caddy crew want you back as soon as possible. How about carrying my bag tomorrow? I've got an important match and sure could use your wisdom.'"

At this point it looked like Mr. Gentry's story to the people under the tree was over, but nobody from the board said anything. Finally, Gentry said, "I'm sorry for going on so long. I suppose you're wondering what all this has to do with Meadows and your project with the kids. But please think about it, *you* future caddies."

Sitting there in the grass under the tree with members of the Fair Are the Meadows church governing board, Pastor Ek's head had been spinning. He wished he had had a note pad to record some of Gentry's key points, but this much was certain. He had a sermon topic for Sunday.

WWJCD?

On the marquee in front of the church, the upcoming Sunday's sermon title was announced as "WWJCD?" Paige said to her mom, "He's got it wrong. It's supposed to be WWJD–What would Jesus do? Like what you see on bumper stickers–Not Jesus Christ."

But Pastor Ek knew what he was doing. On that Sunday after the obligatory announcements and Good Mornings of the day, he paused, aimed his gaze above the congregation, and asked ultra-slowly, "What would Jesus's *caddy* do?" The congregation laughed. Enough of them knew of the caddying project. They prepared themselves for yet another extended g-o-l-f and G-o-d comparison. Not necessarily a bad gig, but there must be a point where the golf analogies wear thin.

Pastor Ek had several scriptural readings that he thought would lay a foundation for what he wanted to get across. The liturgist for the day was once more Jayne Nova. In a perky clear voice that everyone could hear, Ms. Nova read her passages as if they were directed toward a golfer and caddy, like Jesus and someone helping him. She read,

"Phil 2:13 - For it is God which worketh in you both to will and to do of his good pleasure."

"Eccl 4:9 - Two are better than one; because they have a good reward for their labor."

Next Ms. Nova spoke in words that she said could come from the caddy, first to Jesus.

"Ps 18:36 - You gave a wide place for my steps under me, and my feet did not slip."

And then to anyone who would hear.

"Job 23:11 - My foot has held fast to His path; I have kept His way and not turned aside."

At this point pastor Ek took over and read from the gospel of John before moving into his sermon,

"John 13:4-14 He laid aside his outer garments, and taking a towel, tied it around his waist. Then he poured water into a basin and began to wash the disciples' feet and to wipe them with the towel that was wrapped around him. He came to Simon Peter, who said to him, 'Lord, do you wash my feet?' Jesus answered him, 'What I am doing you do not understand now, but afterward you will understand.' Peter said to him, 'You shall never wash my feet.' Jesus answered him, 'If I do not wash you, you have no share with me.'"

Pastor Ek's point was that we all need help and support from others. The weakest among us, of course need to receive, but also give; the strongest need to receive as well as give. Even Jesus who always gives, needs to receive. Jesus's ultimate impact depends on us. He needs us to walk alongside him and share our wisdom and questions.

Toward the end Ek said, "I suspect that you need me, or somebody like me. I can say for sure that I need you."

He closed with, "We are Jesus's caddies. In our enigmatic game with the small ball, caddies are the only ones that can help the player during the heat of competition–during the struggle when it counts. Sometimes people like this are known as Disciples. Apostles. Feet washers. Pin tenders. Bag toters. Not only do we need Jesus, he needs us. And he travels on foot, not in a motorized cart that makes things seem easier than they are. It's better on foot."

Out in the congregation Keyshawn Gentry smiled. The service ended with a musical arrangement of *In the Garden* that had an oboe and flute accompanying guest pianist David Oldman. They did an instrumental first run of the refrain and were then joined by the organ and congregation singing words of the first verse and refrain twice through.

> I come to the garden alone,
> While the dew is still on the roses,
> And the voice I hear falling on my ear
> The Son of God discloses.
>
> *Refrain:*
> And He walks with me, and He talks with me,

He tells me I am His own;

And the joys we share as we tarry there,

None other has ever known.

As it was ending Chris thought, "*I love that song–the words and music– but it's over too soon for me. The song. Life? I'm only 27. What about someone who's 72?*"

As he led the benediction, Pastor Ek was relaxed and eager to shake hands and chat at the back of the sanctuary. He didn't always feel that way about the little ritual that sometimes impressed him as labored and perfunctory. He wished more people would substantively comment on his sermons. He wished more would invite him into their homes. He wished more would recite their first and last names–He hadn't been in Belle Waters long enough to know everyone. But this Sunday he was so upbeat and energized that he saw every handshake, every "Nice job, Pastor," and every member with a blank face and weak hand, as a point of light.

He especially wanted to shake the hands and look into the eyes of two he saw in the pews, Mr. Gentry and Mrs. Ahlgren. For different reasons. He loved that Gentry had returned, and he wanted to somehow express that pleasure. He was still troubled by what he saw as a broken relationship with Joyce Ahlgren, and he wanted to smile at her and try to regain her respect. These hopes were realized, but the memorable moment of the morning came when Jayne–cheekily with no apologies–broke into the line, squeezed his hand especially hard and said, "I'm going to caddy for you. Look for my text message this afternoon."

Pastor Ek's Caddy

Comfortable in the driver's seat of her red Mazda Miata convertible, she showed up at his house at 5:45 a.m. the next morning. Golfer Ek held onto his clubs tightly in the passenger side as they drove to Muni Golf Course on the west side of the river. Ek had to admit to himself that from his first glance weeks before he thought that Jayne Nova was one good-looking woman. This morning "foxy" came to mind. She kept her eyes on the road so he had a long look at her right profile: Chiseled? Roman? Confident? The effect was exciting, confirmed his earlier impressions, and contributed to the edginess that had him tossing and turning during the night. He was worried that his golf game would be pathetic. He wanted to impress this caddy.

Some other early morning golfers had gone out on the front nine and it was a bit bunched up, so Ek and Nova started on number ten, a par five heading north from the clubhouse. Not wanting to pose through a series of practice swings, and committed to avoiding taking a mulligan–another shot from the same spot without counting the first one–Ek was stiff and tense as he teed off with his driver, a club with a head the size of a cantaloupe. Bad results. Had the swing been with an iron, it would have shanked. This so-called "wood"–made of some exotic-sounding inorganic substance designed to maximize distance–contacted the ball with the shaft rather than the face and produced a feeble low slice that kicked up a rooster tail spray of dew fifty yards off the tee. Caddy Nova stifled a laugh that came out as a snort. Ek hit a respectable fairway "metal" for his next shot, and then as they strolled along he launched into a mini-sermon on the duties of caddying, assuming that she had never done it. It felt good to take attention away from his shot-making as he ticked off the usual rules about bag toters' expected behavior on the putting surfaces, in the hazards, and "through the green"– That is, everywhere else. Marching alongside him, she gave the impression of listening intently.

Ek reached the first green after five shots that found him about eight feet from the hole. The grass hadn't been mowed yet, so putts created a visual history. His were embarrassing. He three-putted, and cursed to himself. But something else that had been happening on that hole took his attention away from the pathetic quality of his game. It was Jayne's behavior. She talked and moved around when he was ready to hit shots. She stepped on his intended putting line, which is bad enough under any conditions, but on the soft moist green, the effect was magnified.

And she carried the bag like she was gravity-deprived: out of balance at a funny angle. She didn't get better as the round progressed. Adding insult to injury, she would offer swing change ideas that made Ek shake his head, like encouraging him to strengthen an already strong grip and to try looking at the target rather than the ball on full shots. Really. It almost seemed like she was trying to be a bad caddy.

She was.

It took him a long time to realize it, and even longer to appreciate her motives. On their ninth hole of the morning, she tallied up his score on the card she was keeping. It was two more than he had calculated in his head: a 51 rather than a 49.

"Okay?" she asked.

He considered letting the matter go, but finally said, "I count two less than that. Let me see what you have," and they both acknowledged that she had written down more strokes than he took.

"Well, that's a baby step, anyway," she said.

"Whaddah you mean?"

"You stood up for yourself."

He looked at her.

She went on, "My dear friend, Mr. Rev. Pastor Christopher Hilding Ek, you just accepted and tolerated all my bad caddy acting–I'll bet you thought it was for real. Right? It took wrong numbers to shake you awake."

His brow furrowed.

"Well," she said, "you should speak up for what you think is wrong. I really believe that golf and caddying are frivolous little playthings compared to the real issues of the world, but–and I have to say that I *really* like you a lot so it hurts me to say this–but rules are rules. You gave me rules and then didn't have the b. . ." She almost referred to male anatomy, paused, and said, "Well, you didn't enforce them. What about the big wrongs and exclusions of the day? I haven't known you long enough to see for myself, but I'll bet you keep quiet about them too?"

He flashed back to the blistering he got from Joyce. And now comes this one.

6

Ecstasies & Agonies

A Mellow Calm

THE CADDYING GIG THAT the kids designed succeeded beyond everyone's expectations. Elders and confirmands got to know each other. Well. The quality of golf improved for most of them and the bag toting was downright stellar. That's what Mr. Gentry said, anyway. Nine holes at Muni became a regular event every other early Thursday morning for the original group of board members and kids. Late in the summer, together they hosted a sunrise shotgun scramble and brunch. The entire Fair Are the Meadows congregation was invited along with the Belle Waters Junior Golf Association. Enough players signed up to fill sixteen foursomes. Each included a confirmand, a BWJGA kid, an elder, and another adult. Meadows youngsters prepared and served food highlighted by a deep-dish omelet. Dawn and Don Mearn donated eggs, pastries came from a local bakery, and a farmers' market regular provided veggies.

So, in spite of some little storms, here in his still early tenure at Fair Are the Meadows, rays of sunshine had poked through the clouds over Reverend Christopher Hilding Ek. He and the youth were clicking, his relationship with the board was better, and he knew the names and faces of just about every member. His performance from the pulpit was well-received, attendance on Sunday morning moved from good to great, and the revived church was getting a reputation around town. A pretty good one.

And then there was Jayne. Chris found his thoughts drifting to her a lot, and with it came a tingle of nerves. He was attracted to her–for sure–but she seemed to be playing games with him, like mind games. He knew by now that she also had considerable experience in the game of life called golf including success in junior tournaments years ago.

Her anti-golf screed during that first meeting in his office showed him that she was a devil's advocate and contrarian. Her masquerade as a bumbling caddy was something else. She set him up for that lecture in self-improvement. "*What is she after?*" he asked himself with moist palms and a heartbeat he could see through his shirt, but then he hesitantly concluded "*Good for her. She's a working psychologist and I need analysis. And a caddy.*"

And there was Joyce Ahlgren. She had sent him an email saying she'd go back to teaching Sunday school ("I can't let those little kids down."), but he found it difficult to go back to venerating her as he did before she quit. When they would occasionally run into each other, they were overly nice, quick to give an obligatory compliment, and formal. Artificial, but she was back with the younger kids. A half-full glass.

And the reputation thing. Because of their caddying project, Fair Are the Meadows Family Church was talked about around town as a place where something was happening. (It didn't hurt that Meadows kids and some older members wore t-shirts asking WWJCD?) When Chris was introduced as that still pretty new minister at Fair Are the Meadows Church during a Rotary Club meeting one Tuesday noon, somebody called out, "That's the golfing church. What's your handicap, Reverend?" followed by friendly laughter.

Rev. Ek smiled and thought, "*I'd love to get it to single digits someday.*"

He liked that his church was being talked about, but he wasn't wild about the fact that comments focused more on the golf than the Christian values he was trying to nurture: different generations interacting; people helping each other; playing by the rules; following the behavior of Jesus. He listened to see if Meadows was ever referred to as a country club congregation. He wouldn't like that.

These days his thoughts drifted back to that undergraduate class in social sources of denominationalism and a conclusion he came away with: a homogeneous flock is not necessarily bad. Over the years he had learned of energetic congregations of hunters, motorcyclists, pilots, and cooks. He recently read about a Belle Waters person who was leading a little church in New England based on a pub culture. Beer. A coherent bunch of golfers walking with Jesus was worth developing without too much embarrassment or conflict of interest.

Hands

Hands are critical to successful golf swings, and hands are needed to address homelessness.

Mission Statement of "Helping Hands"

"Our goal is to provide short-term shelter, warmth, protection, and guidance to the least fortunate in our midst, so that they will become more resourceful, self-sustaining, and hopeful."

Several Belle Waters congregations had joined forces to make Helping Hands function, and the contributions from Fair Are the Meadows earned high praise. A ready supply of members made beds, cooked meals, read to children, and did other tasks that are supposed to make homeless families feel welcome and secure during their residencies at the churches. Some Meadows members slept all night on site without complaining as they responded to late doorbells or telephone calls that interrupted their sleep. Others patiently listened to tales of woe. Sometimes the efforts of Meadows members resulted in employment for a guest or opened doors to a more long-term housing arrangement. Many members quietly gave cash and things to the families that found shelter at the church, before bidding them farewell as they moved on to their next port of call. The Helping Hands efforts at Meadows were seen as a model of how to do it.

Joyce Ahlgren was one of the tireless volunteers. She stood out as judged not only by the time she committed, but also through the quality of her relationships with the families. She spent hours listening to their stories. She filled in for members who couldn't make it to their assigned role. She slipped guests coupons, cash, and checks. She communicated with them after they left Meadows for other ports in new storms. They sang praises of her. That saint.

To somebody who didn't know her, Mrs. Ahlgren sometimes came across as one who didn't care what she looked like. The result seemed right and true and beautiful to those who did. Her looks as well as her manner projected understated grace and empathy. She listened to her kids, her church friends, strangers. Everyone. She worked hard at Sunday school teaching, gardening, home making, and her dedication to the down and out. Joyce Ahlgren confronted life head-on without any pretense or hidden agenda. She was a natural.

Paige Ahlgren reluctantly accompanied her mother during the weeks when the church would host the homeless guests. She never came right out and said that she didn't like coming along, but Joyce could read Paige's body language. However, she–Joyce–kept quiet. Paige *was there* as often as any kid from the congregation, and that's something to be thankful for.

But unbeknownst to her mother or anyone else, Paige's preoccupation with homelessness was growing, and festering. Soon after the caddying project got on its feet, Paige launched a fiery, new crusade. She was not subtle about where she aimed the flame of her bazooka: at her mother and Pastor Ek. "This church doesn't really do *anything* meaningful for the homeless," she said after calling them together for a dressing down. "The only benefit comes to your conscience. We members of Meadows should take homeless people into our homes. It's as simple as that!"

A Fascinating Foursome

Jayne Nova was always quick to volunteer for Helping Hands tasks, and she told people that one of the reasons she started coming to the church was because of what it did for homeless families. When Jayne heard about what she called Paige's recent fit of righteous indignation, she rolled her eyes and said to Chris, "Poor Joyce," and then launched into a critique of Joyce's daughter as she and Chris were driving to the golf course for an early Monday morning nine holes.

When they were on the fifth hole Chris just happened to glance over at the first tee and stopped in his tracks. Paired together and getting ready to hit their drives were the Guy-By-the-Stop-Sign and the Guy-From-the-Confluence. Chris watched as they hit irons to stay short of the water hazard, slung their bags over their shoulders, and headed south at a brisk clip. His jaw had dropped enough for Jayne to ask what was the matter.

"Those men are homeless," he said. "And they're out here playing golf . . ."

". . . That rich man's game," she interrupted, and pursed her lips.

Chris and Jayne stayed quiet as they played out the hole and headed for the sixth tee. They both hit their best drives of the day on the par 5 dogleg, and then the Reverend broke their silence: "My head's spinning."

Jayne said, "You do have a silly look on your face. What's up?"

Chris told the story of how he had met each of those homeless guys, and then suggested that Jayne and he wait around the clubhouse after nine holes to grab a bite to eat with them. Jayne was uncharacteristically closed mouthed, but soon she suggested that she and Chris have a little putting competition on the practice green while waiting. They did. She creamed him.

Chris's two acquaintances walked from the ninth green toward the tenth tee without stopping. Jayne said, "Aren't you going to call to them? They didn't see us." Chris still didn't react, so Jayne yelled, "Hey guys! Coffee? With us!" The Guy-By-the-Stop-Sign and the Guy-From-the-Confluence looked back at her and then at each other. They pointed at Chris, and walked toward him and Jayne.

It was awkward. In the past Chris had talked to each of them at length–Stop Sign several times and that one memorable session with Confluence when Chris snapped awake from the dream–but he didn't know their names.

Jayne motioned for them to go into the clubhouse and they sat together at a table for four over by the north window. Jayne said, "You know, I'm really hungry. I'm having a burger basket and large Coke. How about you guys? It's on me." Stop-Sign and Confluence had the same as Jayne. Chris ordered an Arnold Palmer and a bag of crispy Cheetos.

The Reverend Ek knew that he should take the lead in talking, but he was torn about how to begin. He wanted to get into their backgrounds regarding golf, but felt tongue-tied. The four of them just looked at each other for a painfully long time while the food was being prepared. After a brow-furrowing glance at Chris, Jayne saved the moment. She said, "What do you think about the water hazards out here? I kinda like them." Confluence perked up and went into a lengthy critique of these features including what he called the drainage structure.

Jayne was expecting them to tell how they avoided hitting balls into water or sad tales about how they didn't. Instead she heard Confluence's knowledge of hydrology, landscaping, and aesthetics. Golf course design. "*This guy knows golf*"! she thought.

Chris and Stop Sign were quiet. Chris was relieved that Jayne and Confluence yakked on and on after the food arrived. They–the four of them–never did exchange names that day. As soon as Confluence and Stop Sign left to play the back nine Chris gasped, "Why on earth would homeless guys play golf?"

Jayne looked at him for a moment, getting her thoughts together. "I'm kind of surprised at your words, but why not?"

Chris shot back, "Literally, these guys are mired in the deepest of pits and they have the time and resources to go golfing? It boggles the mind."

"Uh, Reverend Ek . . . haven't we had a conversation like this before, back in your office when *I* was criticizing golf? I said it was a game for the wealthy, and you jumped all over me. I'm not surprised at all that these guys golf."

They locked eyes.

"Do you really understand this game?" she said.

"No, I'm just a learner."

"Well, aren't we all, but let me say this: Golf is for getting away from the cares of the world, for a while anyway. Like going to the movies during the Great Depression. If you really are into golf, you don't think about other things when you're out there. Out here."

"Please continue," Chris said.

"When you're golfing you're in that bubble and at the extreme, it's like a sweet addiction–a magnificent obsession–but do you know what the key is?"

"I guess not."

"It's hope. Every serious golfer has a dream of playing all the time like she does when she's at her best. You know what that means, right?"

"What?"

"She's *thinks* she's good enough to be a pro or at least a big shot amateur. I bet these guys–Confluence and Stop Sign or whatever you call them–feel that way. Golf can be a way out. Have you ever heard the story of Moe Norman, that Canadian?"

Chris said, "Yeah, I think so, a little bit. Wasn't he on the Asperger's Spectrum? Keyshawn mentions him once in a while. That guy who hit from his chosen groove on an iron every time?"

Jayne said, "Yeah. He had so much control of his game that he would hit a wedge first on a par four and then go for the green with a driver. No tee, of course. Phenomenal. Do you realize that he lived in his car, a big old Buick, for months at a time? He was homeless. That's what they say, anyway."

Heart to Heart

Driving Chris home Jayne said, "I enjoyed that. The time with your friends, and the golf."

Chris stayed quiet.

"Well, didn't *you*?" she prompted.

Chris didn't know where to begin. He finally said, "I don't take criticism very well. I tell other people to let me know where I screw up or miss something obvious, but when they do, it bothers me more than it should."

"Like what? Give me an example."

"Well, the way you looked at me after I didn't introduce those guys. I know what you were thinking."

"What?"

"That I should have known their names. Right?"

"Sure, but it's no big deal."

"Well, it is to me. I don't know how to deal with this homeless stuff. Maybe I haven't asked their names because I didn't want to get too close to them. They are not 'my friends.'" Then defensively, he said, "You know, we're not supposed to intrude on their lives. A cardinal rule for Helping Hands is to not ask personal questions of the guests."

Jayne and Chris stayed quiet the rest of the drive. With the Mazda still idling he hoisted his clubs and said, "Thanks for the ride. I've got work to do–a sermon in my head that's screaming to get out."

She blew him a kiss, and drove off. That little gesture . . . She may not have thought about it before, during, or afterwards, but Chris did. *"What's with this woman? I think about her a lot."* He laughed to himself when he acknowledged that in two settings where he should be utterly focused–playing golf and delivering a sermon–if she is there, he can't take his mind off her. *"She is so much fun to be around, but she's a challenge. Anything but a pushover. My seminary buddies said women would be coming at me from all directions–especially the single ones but others too–so be prepared and get ready to 'handle them.' This Jayne, though. She's a mystery. In a good way, but am I ready to take it on? To take* her *on? Do I have any control over it? Yipes!"*

And an old Andrews Sisters song he had heard at his grandparents' home popped into his head: It starts out "You call everybody darling', and everybody calls you darling' too . . ." and then the words go on to warn about the consequences of gratuitous affection. He thought *"Kisses are more powerful than words. To me they are. I wonder how often she gives them out?"*

A Big Sermon

Usually when Chris returned from Monday morning golf, he felt physically fulfilled. His arms and legs and back and chest would be stretched and relaxed. His mind would be clear. His breathing invigorated. His hands strong. He would be ready to concentrate on things other than the next shot's possibilities or the last shot's disappointment. This is not to say that golf ever left his awareness or lost its absolute importance, but if a round had finished respectfully–not with a hope-sapping triple bogey or worse on the last hole–he could move unhindered to other important things for a while.

This Monday, in spite of Jayne's kiss and a confidence-building ninth hole par capped off by his sinking a lovely left to right ten-foot putt that led to a wholly respectable 44, he was anything but relaxed post-golf. As soon as he got in the door, he went to his computer and started drafting a sermon for the coming Sunday. Its working title: "Leveling with you-out-there-in-the-pews . . . and God."

Planning sermons was therapy for Pastor Chris. Homilies hovering in the recesses of his memory would start humming as their–he called it–character took shape and their performance day neared. Typing the first few words made it real. This day his fingers began with, "In academia, I discovered that issues and insights, commonplace among scholars, are viewed as highly controversial and even as heresy in the churches. . . ."

The particular issues that he wanted to explore via "Leveling with you . . ." were what he called big ones. Big to him anyway: candor and homelessness. He knew he wasn't on top of either, but if this sermon were to serve him the way most others had, he would at least learn something. He took comfort from that adage that is meant to encourage new schoolteachers: "Your pupils *might* learn something by a lesson that you teach. You *will*." Rev. Ek's parishioners *might* learn from the Leveling sermon. He *would*.

During the awkward meal earlier out at the golf course, Chris felt a shiver realizing how little he knew about where he wanted his church to go regarding homelessness. The golfing guys brought it to life and that scared him. On the ride home, he realized how unprepared he was to talk directly with his congregation about that or anything. It was so hard for him to say what he thought.

Interestingly, Chris was raised by a mother who counseled him to say what you think. Be candid. Get it out in the open. Don't let your real feelings fester deep in your heart (She used those exact words). Frankness may hurt in the short run, but you'll be glad down the road. It's better to share too much information than not enough, and it's better to tell too much about what's going on in your own head and heart. Don't worry about how people react.

Intellectually, Chris knew that this was sound advice and in some settings, he could practice it, like with his young pupils in Chicago and here in Belle Waters. He told them:

"Let me know what's bothering you.

"Don't hold back.

"Criticize me and my sermons. Hold my feet to the fire.

"Analyze the scriptures. Don't be afraid to point out contradictions or silliness.

This practice with the kids was a gentle variation on the brutal candor that had characterized gatherings called "Friday Lunches" in Chicago when Chris got together with a few other seminarians, all unmarried guys. They voiced things that he wouldn't dream of saying from the pulpit or anywhere else. Like,

"Most of the Old Testament's so-called heroes were jerks. Abraham, David, Samson. All those old men."

"And from the New Testament: '. . . those twelve bleating sheep, the apostles.' Even the big Number One took a hit: 'Jesus never took a shower. Imagine the BO.'"

[Referring to laity] "It's us and them, baby. Don't let them get to you, those alligators."

[Responding to a tearful announcement from one of them to the group:] "So your dad has cancer. Get over it. He's going to die, but go to heaven. Right? (sigh) Or not? . . . Not!"

And they would talk about their brushes with sex in the parish. Like awkward moments they experienced during internships. About married women who came on to them, or who *seemed* to anyway. "Those lingering eyes and tempting thighs," one of the guys offered. "Those breathless references to problems in marriages when they looked up at me after staring at their folded hands. Those allusions to intimacy gone bad." Years later Chris concluded that his buddies back then represented a broad range of youthful sexual experience, but the ones who talked about it the most had to have known the least. Chris knew something back then, but he had a lot to learn.

Many of these snippets of candor would end with the lads laughing, but they kept quiet the time one of them announced, sheepishly, "I'm more of a fundamentalist than I thought." To a person the others admitted that they were too.

As he typed away at "Leveling . . ." Chris thought back to that ironic little scene when ostensibly liberal future ministers admitted that they had values that overlapped with their fundamentalist [Read: inferior] counterparts. At the time, Chris didn't like the way the Friday Lunch bunch made fun of 'Fundies,' but he never said anything about it. Then as now he knew he should take a chance at saying what he believed–damn the reactions–but so far, he hadn't brought himself to do it when the opportunities arose, and what he recognized as a nagging little problem during his seminary years was throbbing away now during his first year in the pulpit. Chris wanted this sermon to be a bold gesture that would help his people get to know him better.

He smiled as he thought about John Shelby Spong, that outspoken retired bishop of the Episcopal Church. Chris thought, *"Paige Ahlgren thinks this guy's the answer to our problems and Elder Stone claims Spong's not even a Christian. And I'm the pastor of both of them."*

Early in Chris's time at Fair Are the Meadows, he had briefly referenced Spong in a sermon. Afterwards in the narthex Elder Eberhard Stone shook his hand [too hard], looked him in the eye and–dripping with attitude–said, "Remember my young friend, this place is affiliated with The United Church *of Christ*, not with those eggheads or whomever you bow down to at liberal seminaries like Chicago. We are the United Church *of Christ*, and we're called that for a reason. We could be the church of Jesus, but it's Christ! Please don't upset my Sunday mornings with Spong. I've read his stuff and it's [Stone paused and chose his words carefully] . . . well it's not what I need to confirm my faith." Pastor Ek had a response all set to fire back, but kept his mouth shut.

Spong claims that most popular interpretations of Christian scripture are not sustainable and do not speak to the situation of modern communities. He supports an approach to scripture–informed by scholarship and compassion–which he says can be consistent with both Christian tradition and contemporary understandings of the universe. This is hardly controversial in most UCC churches these days, but there are people out in the pews–like Mr. Stone–with differing views clinging to traditional renditions of Virgin Birth. Resurrection. Life ever after. The Triune God. Jesus as God. The fundamentals.

Pastor Ek was reluctant to present scripture as boldly non-traditional as did Bishop Spong, partly because he really did feel that there was some sacrilege in Spong's words, but he laughed out loud when he also realized that he didn't want Elder Stone's bad breath settling over him after the service when they would lock hands. So, he settled on starting out by serving the congregation words that were a mixture of lemonade and ice tea punch with a few drops of vodka poured in on the sly. An Arnold Palmer on steroids.

When the big Sunday arrived, Chris decked himself out in a black robe and clerical collar, something he hadn't done since his ordination service. And *he* read the liturgy. Jayne Nova threw him a mock pout when Chris announced that he was taking over the liturgical duties for the day. Pastor Ek read:

"From Ps 25:5 Lead me in your truth and teach me, for you are the God of my salvation; for you I wait all the daylong.

"From Ps 43:3 Send out your light and your truth; let them lead me; let them bring me to your holy hill and to your dwelling!

"From Ps 86:11 Teach me your way, O Lord, that I may walk in your truth; unite my heart to fear your name."

Without comment he moved to the New Testament and read:

"From Jas 1:18 Of his own will He [Jesus Christ] brought us forth by the word of truth, that we should be a kind of first fruits of his creatures."

Then Reverend Ek stopped, paused, looked his congregation in the eye, and asked, "Have *you* accepted Jesus as your truth? Your Savior?"

It was so quiet you could have heard an owl blink.

Ek continued, "Well, let me say a few words about a friend of mine who responded with a yes. While growing up, the question that I just asked you was a call that he heard from the pulpit again and again. Finally, at a revival service, he walked down the aisle and told the preacher 'I love Jesus and believe in Him and want to accept him as my personal savior.' Now these days he is a professor that some would call agnostic or even atheistic. He stays in touch with his salvation experience by writing fiction that never makes light of that premature conversion."

Looking out at a high school English teacher in his congregation, Pastor Ek pounded on the pulpit but whispered, "Some of the most important truths in our world come from fiction, and they are partners with the Biblical stories. They sometimes *are* the Biblical stories. The Bible is full of stories and we–you and I and others–make new stories out of them. We swim in the sweet cooling waters of fiction.

"You and I and everyone know that we can't resist stories. They are glue that holds us together over time. So, whose stories should we cling to? Theologians'? (One congregant called out 'no.'). My friend's? (looking back at the teacher). Yours (looking at Paige Ahlgren)? Yours (looking at Eberhard Stone)? Or maybe yours? (For the first time, he looked right at three men who were strangers to most people of the congregation: Keyshawn, Stop Sign, and Confluence.) Or maybe mine?"

With a big grin, Paige called out "Noooo," and everyone laughed. Including Pastor Chris.

Paige was sitting next to Jayne in the same pew as the three men. Ek smiled as he thought of them as a golfing five-some, four amateurs and their pro, Keyshawn Gentry.

Ek brought the sermon to a close, "A seminarian classmate of mine thinks that anything that begins to give people a sense of their own worth and dignity is God. And he tells it in fiction that he writes and recites. I kinda like that idea. No, I mean I like that idea, unqualified. To be continued . . . Amen."

At this point the Reverend Christopher Hilding Ek felt great and vigorously sang the post sermon hymn he had chosen for the day: "*What a Friend We Have in Jesus*," and he enthusiastically led the time of Joys & Concerns that invited pew sitters to speak about the highs and lows of their week. Usually, Chris's role in this very personal part of the service was to summarize comments as he worked them into a closing prayer. He did that, but added his own two cents worth in referring back to his sermon: "I just got something big off my back, and I feel good. Thank you, Lord."

After the benediction and march back up the aisle to a rousing organ rendition of "*Now Thank We All Our God*," he positioned himself for shaking hands with his worshippers in the narthex, but they turned out to be more restrained than he expected. His heart was beating so hard he could feel it rustling his robe. They were straight-faced. Tamped down. *He* was excited. Why weren't they?

Jayne was next-to-last in the queue that had moved along quicker than usual. Looking him in the eye and softly scratching the palm of his outstretched hand with her fingernail, she said "We gotta talk." And then moved on.

Paige was last. She shook his hand formally and said, "We gotta talk. Can I come in to see you tomorrow morning? Whoops, I mean afternoon.

I know you always golf on Monday early." Mouth half open, he nodded. Before he could get any words out, she had moved on.

Keyshawn, Confluence, and Stop Sign weren't in line. Chris had hoped they would be. Eberhard Stone wasn't there either. For once, Chris had wanted to shake his hand and say, "What did you think of that sermon?" Stone would have *had* to like it. It was for him. One side of Chris felt guilty in preparing sermons with a particular pew sitter in mind, but he found out from his seminary classmates that they all do it sometimes.

Feedback

As was his habit, Chris didn't look at his accumulated post-Sunday sermon emails until he returned from the golf course the next day. He never knew what to expect. There could be praise: "You hit the jackpot! I loved every word. Thanks for all you do." Questions: "What did your reading really mean? Why don't you like the Gospel of John?" Sometimes there would be suggestions for what he should refer to in the future: "The book of Revelation, Fred Craddock's sermons, Marilynne Robinson's latest novel, Krista Tippett's interview from yesterday, Martin Luther, Martin Luther King, Jr."

So far at Fair Are the Meadows church, the negative comments aimed at Chris seemed few, far between, and minor tweaks. He thought most of them kind of silly: "You should walk up the side aisle. Please sing louder during the hymns (You have a good voice). Thank the custodian regularly. He's a pillar of this church!"; but once in a while a comment would get to him: "Be more forceful in asking us to increase our pledges. Don't sweat so much. Don't fiddle with your fingers when you talk. Are you a conservative? Are you a Democrat?" Silly or not, they stuck with him like dreams that proclaim: "Think about these things more!"

This particular Monday he was especially interested in what sparklers would be waiting. He expected there would be at least three–Jayne, Paige, and Stone–but there was only one. It was a phone call from Keyshawn Gentry that said, "I thought you gave an interesting sermon yesterday, and so did my pals. Let's get together. I have some interesting new thoughts about your swing. In the meantime, watch Bryson DeChambeau on the Golf Channel."

Chris thought, "*Interesting? When somebody is too polite to blatantly say negative things about a player's swing, they often use that word.*"

The message from his golf mentor moved him to reach for one of the putters leaning against his desk and stroke some balls that had been waiting in the corner section of his office where he had finally constructed a practice green, but as he rose from his chair he noticed a letter-sized envelope that had been slipped under the door. It was addressed to "Pastor C" with "Paige" in the upper left corner. His heart raced as he unsuccessfully looked for a letter opener and finally tore it open. A hand-written essay began,

"It's better to give than to receive: Acts 20:35"

Chris's first thought was that in that passage Jesus says, "It's more *blessed* to give . . ." but realized that he was being reflexively anal. *Hey, this is a letter hand-written–cursive no less–from a kid that I thought was co-opted by things digital.* He relaxed a little.

Paige's words continued,

> *"Sitting there in the pews yesterday I noticed the friendly face of your golfing guru Keyshawn, and two of his pals who had to be homeless guys. I'm not just guessing here. I've seen them with him at the golf course and, let me tell you Pastor C, their humble, tattered, and unwashed clothes and ancient, battered car filled with the booty of a hoarder, give them away, but they do play with decent clubs and the quality of their golf is down-right impressive. I've watched them tee off ahead of me, and I've seen them hit full shots when they're off in the distance. Those guys know what they're doing. Their grips are fundamentally sound, their swings have rhythm and integrity, and their shots are, . . . well, you would love to hit balls like they do. No offence, Pastor C, but either those guys could whip your ass.*
>
> *"Now you may wonder why I am writing a letter about golf the day after what–behind your back–some of us have been calling your coming out sermon. Well, I learned from that sermon, and I have to share it with you. Here goes. Your bit about candor flew out at me and I'm trying to put it into practice now right here. Why should I use fake polite language when I mean something that is best said by straight talk? Seriously, those homeless guys are good golfers and they really could beat you regularly, but you are trying, and when you start to play better than they do, I will acknowledge it in equally direct language. So, you encouraged candor, and I am practicing it here.*
>
> *"But the main thing I took from your sermon is what you didn't say and could have. You didn't even touch on homeless-ness, and I totally suspect that you knew that you had homeless people out there in the congregation listening to you. And I bet*

that as you read this you are thinking 'I prepare my sermons in advance. I can't change them on the spot.'

"But you can. You could have and you should have. This is the end of my scolding, Pastor C. because I have something much more important to share with you, an idea that has been sloshing around in my mind and spilled out yesterday morning as I nervously squirmed in the pew: Those homeless guys have something to give us! I think that when individuals or congregations try to help each other, they may be—probably are—forgetting that wonderful advice from Jesus: It's better to give (etc.). Are you following me?

"I suppose everyone knows that I am a wise guy, gal. I admit it. When I was very young I had a birthday party where I expected, and got, lots of gifts. When my mother, that broad-cum-saint that you and everybody around here worship, suggested that I should give one of my gifts to each of my siblings that evening, I objected and didn't do it. Mom would never force me to do something, but I wish she had that time. Guilt set in when the next party I went to had the birthday kid—the celebrated one who is supposed to be receiving presents—lecturing us in the invitation "No gifts!" and then during the party she gave us stuff. Not expensive, but thoughtful. Everybody loved it and her and said very kind things about her. They meant it. She deserved it. I felt kinda funny at the time and didn't sincerely thank her, but over time it grew on me what a great gesture that was. It is better to give than receive! I am a latecomer to practicing this advice, but I do realize that something warm and good can result. Can come to the giver. Those guys can give golfing lessons!"*

Shanks

Paige's letter had Chris all excited. So much so that he temporarily forgot something scary: The night before he had a horrible dream where he could only "shank" golf shots, and then his dream came to life as he started doing it out there today at Muni. Shanking is where the ball squirts off the hosel of the club and sails or dribbles almost at right angles from the intended line of flight. Most serious golfers will acknowledge that a shank is the worst possible outcome from trying to hit a shot, worse than a "whiff" which is an onomatopoeic euphemism for a total miss. But a whiff is almost always followed by a next shot that somehow contacts the ball, and a whiff doesn't get into a player's head. The cause of a whiff seems to be explainable and fixable. Shanks appear out of the blue with no warning. The cause of a shank is debated, and so are the potential cures, but one thing is certain: When golfers start shanking, they become paralytic over the ball the next time they try to hit it, while praying that it won't happen again.

In short, shanks affect golfers mentally, destroying their confidence. Like this:

An Augustana College golf team player, Poddy Carlson, was finishing off a phenomenal first nine in a match at Indian Bluff, near the Quad Cities. He recalls, "I was five under par after eight holes. My drive on the short par four ninth was twenty yards shy and to the right of the green. My confidence couldn't have been higher. An up and down would give me another hole under par and a 29. Wow! But, instead I started shanking. Three shanks, a chip, and two putts added up to a seven. Still a very nice nine holes–two under par–if you just look at the numbers, but disappointing and then some. I had only one swing thought the entire back nine: Keep every ounce of weight on my heels. I didn't shank again that day but the confidence and good swing vanished. I shot 42 or 43. My main memory of that day is of the shanks and what they did to me."

Shanks can afflict professional golfers in the heat of competition. Jack Nicklaus was playing in the 1964 Masters as the defending champion. As he waited to hit his full shot to the difficult par 3 twelfth, he noticed the co-founders of Augusta National, Bobby Jones and Clifford Roberts, sitting in a cart in front and to the right of the tee. He was standing there with an eight-iron in his hands. The pin was back right. He shanked it over their heads. It went so far right it didn't even go in the water.

And at the 1972 Bing Crosby National Pro-Am, Johnny Miller was on the downhill par-4 16th hole at Pebble Beach in the final round, tied with Nicklaus. Everybody thought the 32-year-old Golden Bear, with 36 victories, would devour the brash, 24-year-old Miller, but that's not what happened. *The shank devoured Miller.* After a perfect drive Miller sized up his approach shot and, using a seven-iron, hit what he later called "the perfect shank." He bogeyed the hole, lost in a playoff and left the Monterey peninsula a changed man. A year later, when Miller won the U.S. Open at Oakmont, he played the inward half of his final-round 63 with one swing thought: Don't shank it. After the Crosby, he never led another tournament without it playing on his mind down the stretch.

In response to his own shanking afflictions in the past, Chris Ek would seek help from one of his Bibles: Harvey Penick's *Little Red Book*.

This iconic teacher points his readers toward improving their ball place-ment, head position, or eyesight. Teasingly, he avoids the word shank, replacing it with the softer expression, "Lateral shot." But even Penick left room for doubt in his recipe for success. He would hedge with something like, I *don't think* you can hit it laterally if you follow this advice. Not much confidence registered there.

Tsunamis

That tsunami of shank thoughts rolled over Chris as he finished reading Paige's letter. Now he had a headache, and he wondered, "*Why did I have that terrible golf dream last night? And why did it play out on the golf course this morning–I wasn't thinking about shanking or not shanking when I started doing it? Consciously anyway. Was the dream trying to tell me what really happened Sunday morning? I was so convinced that the sermon was going to be a smash hit–and at first, I thought it was–that I didn't anticipate a tepid response from the congregation. I wasn't ready for that. It was a big deal gone bad, . . . that attempt at leveling with my people and God. Like a promising round of golf side-swiped by lateral shots.*"

And then he remembered the recorded phone message waiting for him from Keyshawn Gentry. He called back and they met later that morn-ing at the Community Center. After shaking hands while sharing quick little smiles, they looked at each other, awkwardly. Chris was ready to break the spell when his teacher said, "Something's bothering you, right." It was a statement, not a question.

With a nervous little crackle in his voice, Chris said, "I've started shanking."

Gentry laughed. Loud and long. Then he said, "Good grief, that's noth-ing. We can fix it for sure. It's only a game. Golf." To himself he said, "*Whew. I thought something serious was bothering Pastor Chris.*"

But Ek was thinking, *I put all that shank stuff at seven or eight on a pain scale. I'll bet he'd rank it a two or three. Or one. Or zero.*" Gentry doesn't feel my pain. It was the first negative reaction he had ever privately voiced about his teacher.

"Anything else?" Gentry said.

Chris sat mute for what seemed like a minute, and then asked, "What did you and your friends think of my sermon yesterday?"

Gentry went quiet again, cupping his chin in both hands. Finally, he said, "Where to begin . . ." along with another pause. And then, "You talked about candor. Telling it like it is, and all that stuff. Good stuff."

Chris waited, and then said, "Well, did you get anything out of it? Did your buddies?"

More silence. Then Gentry said, "We talked about it. A long time. We heard you. They heard you. That's not the best way to say it. They heard *what you didn't say!* I'm trying to be delicate here."

"What do you mean?"

"Well, word had got out that you were going to do a big sermon on Sunday. Something out of the ordinary. Daring. One where visitors could get to really know you and Fair Are the Meadows. I love that name. Okay, I don't think I'm betraying confidences by saying that it was Ms. Nova who mentioned what she thought your sermon plan for Sunday might be. I ran into her down at a coffee shop downtown. I think it was Thursday. She was sitting alone, and I came in to get some pastries to take away. She caught my eye and motioned for me to sit with her. She got right down to business and said, 'How's your student doing?' meaning you. I said fine or something like that and she said, 'Do you know that a couple of your homeless golfing friends and I had a bite to eat together with Pastor Chris at the Muni clubhouse?'

"I nodded and debated whether to say more. My 'golfing friends' [Gentry's fingers made curly signs in the air] had told me about sitting down with you and Ms. Nova out at the golf course, but they were especially interested in what your church is doing with homelessness."

Chris felt faint.

Gentry went on. "Well, they and Ms. Nova thought your sermon would be about homelessness. About guys like them. Maybe even them in particular. I don't think she'd mind my saying this: She thought you might preach about something that goes beyond Helping Hands. They had expectations, she and the guys. You and I have talked about how our expectations can affect how we golf and what we think about and what we do." Keyshawn Gentry was sounding pedantic and preachy.

Chris nodded.

Gentry went on. "Sorry, but I have to add this while I'm throwing stuff at you. Those golfing friends told me something else that we–they and I–chuckled about at first. They said you don't know their names even though you have talked to them quite a bit. Then one of them sighed, 'He's a pastor and he doesn't know our names.'

"Do you know their names, Chris?"

"No, not really."

"What do you call them, to yourself or to Ms. Nova?"

Biting his lower lip Chris said, "I call them Stop Sign and Confluence."

Gentry's look turned serious. His friends were being demeaned. Not taken seriously. He felt a change in his gut as he thought, It's *like calling me boy.'* He said, "They're Alan Mueller and Carleton Stark." Chris was wondering which one was which, but before he figured it out, Gentry said, "Mr. Mueller is the one you call Stop Sign and Mr. Stark is, . . . what did you say you call him? Confluence?"

Chris sat there and took it. Gentry went on about expectations. How they are so powerful in everything we do. Certainly, in golf. In planning shots. In practicing. In designing holes. In applying gamesmanship in a match. And way beyond golf: in a teacher's attitude toward learners, in parents about their kids. And in what ministers expect from their parishioners. Like are they going to be intelligent? Aware? Outspoken? Informed? Critical? Receptive? Asleep? Sheep? . . . The parishioners.

Gentry's comments could have come out of the mouth of Shivas Irons or Bishop Spong.

He finished in a whispering crescendo, "Do you hear me, Chris?" And then looking upward, "Do you hear me, God? Am I making sense? Hey, is anyone out there. Speak up. Please." And he smiled in silence.

The learner nodded.

Gentry had started to calm down inside as he added, "Well, my pastor and friend, the expectations of a lot of us in the pews yesterday were not realized. I can't speak for everyone, but I have talked to Jayne, Alan, Carleton, and Paige . . .

"You talked to Paige about this? What did she say?" Chris thought back to Paige's closing remarks.

Gentry started quoting the young Ms. Ahlgren: "It's better to give than receive. . ." "Well, Mr. Stark and Mr. Mueller have something to give to all of us: golf lessons and more, much more. They are clever guys. Survivors. They could teach, and I know they would, without expecting anything in return, but, and this is a big point, we golfers who would receive their generosity would certainly give them something in return that would be from the heart and not charity. We would be giving to each other? You follow? Does it make sense? It does to Paige Ahlgren."

Ek said to Gentry, "Paige did give me food for thought. She's a good kid. Sometimes people are too hard on her. Yeah, she comes across as a know it all, but her heart is in the right place." He left it at that. His head was foggy as he thanked teacher Gentry for his wisdom and left the Community Center, but through the mist came a little ray of light: *"He called me his pastor!"*

And like the experience of many ministers who want to make up for a failed sermon by re-doubling their efforts as they plan for next time, scripture readings floated into his consciousness. The start of a make-up sermon. *"I'll get it down. I'll do better."*

He heard echoes of passages that had moved him in the past.

"The Lord will never abandon us. Be determined and confident. Do not be afraid . . . Your God, the Lord himself, will be with you. He will not fail you or abandon you. – Deut 31:6

"The Lord chose us to carry out his work. I brought you from the ends of the earth; I called you from its farthest corners and said to you, 'You are my servant.' I did not reject you, but chose you. – Isa 41:9

"The Lord will show us the right way. Trust in the Lord with all your heart. Never rely on what you think you know. Remember the Lord in everything you do, and he will show you the right way. – Prov 3:5-6

"The Lord's approval creates hope. We also boast of our troubles, because we know that trouble produces endurance, endurance brings God's approval, and his approval creates hope. – Rom 5:4"

But this bleak Monday turned worse. He couldn't get into the church when he returned from seeing Gentry. He had misplaced his keys and everything was locked up over the noon hour. He thought of calling Sandy or Ebby Stone or Joyce Ahlgren or somebody else who should have a key, but decided that that would be too humiliating so he went for a walk downtown and headed toward the stateline and the confluence. As soon as he turned south along the river it, he looked ahead and could see that Stop Sign–Mueller–was not sitting in his usual spot. So, disappointed, he changed his route, crossed over the bridge to the west side of the river, and sauntered north on Cliff Street to the Senior Center. Right away, a Meadows member caught his eye and effusively introduced him to others:

"This is our still-new minister. We call him Pastor Chris."

"I hear you're quite a golfer," one woman replied and did a rendition of a swing without a club.

"Oh, I try, but that's even tougher than being a new minister, if you know what I mean." Chris was friendly and engaging.

"I do," she said. "I really do. I keep trying at golf. (Then with a sigh) What is there that keeps me at that devilish game?" Chris shook his head horizontally and smiled.

After a cup of coffee and graciously refusing an offer to stay for lunch, he walked back to church, and confronted evidence that the trials of golf are petty compared to those in his day job. Sandy was back in her office. She greeted him with, "I slipped something under your door. I've been working on it for a while."

Chris replied, "I lost my keys. How about letting me in there?"

As he entered, an envelope stared up at him like a rotten white fish. It was addressed to "Pastor. C" with "Sandy" in the upper left-hand corner. Inside were two sheets of paper with a list headed: *Things we you have to move on.* Black bullets separated them. Chris once told his youth group that he preferred to call them "olives". Bullets are so aggressive.

- Printer ink costs us way too much. Should we cut back on copying?

- The air conditioner in my office isn't working.

- Mrs. Johnson from Eighth Street slipped on some dog pooh on our sidewalk. She is not a happy camper. What should I tell her?

- Eberhard Stone wants to talk to you. He sounds upset.

- Mr. Thorne's stepmother is very ill. It sounds like he was expecting you to visit her in the hospital over the weekend. He wasn't in church yesterday but said he assumed that his family's–he called it–crisis would have been mentioned in the time of Joys and Concerns, but he says it wasn't "according to what people told me." He said you knew about it.

- You got a call from a professor from Chicago. She said that the paper you were co-writing was rejected by *Christian Century* and that she'd get back to you about the details via email.

- You missed a committee meeting this morning. I think it's one of those community projects you joined, but the message was unclear and they didn't leave a callback number. Was it on your calendar?

- You've been invited to a fund-raising golf event at the Country Club on the first Monday of next month. I didn't see any mention of covering your cost (They used to do that for ministers.).

Then in her own hand.

> "Pastor Chris: Please don't forget to visit people in the hospital or home-bounds. They expect you to. Some think you spend too much time on the golf course, when you should be on calls. I hesitate to say this, but it's the cruel truth–the fact that there are people out there who think that. Not me!!!
>
> "[I've been struggling on how to say this next bit.] I am hereby requesting a leave of absence. I need time to think over some issues. Do we need to bring this to the board? I'm sorry.
>
> "Sandy
>
> "P. S. Don't forget that you told everyone you would look into the boiler problems that are bound to hit us when the cold weather comes. I know that's a long way off, but time flies. Sorry for this leave of absence. I have enjoyed working with you. Please speak only in generalities when people ask why I left. It's

more complicated than I care to put in writing now. I might be
back some day, but who knows."

The full force from these gathering clouds would hit him in a while. For the moment, he smiled and thought "*Golf is not this tough. I can live with shanks–lateral shots,*" as the lilt of a favorite old hymn filled his head:

> Time, like an ever-rolling stream,
> Bears all of us away;
> We fly forgotten, as a dream
> Dies at the opening day.

Sweating with a rapid heart, he wondered how they will remember him around here? He thought back to that sweet little sermon early in his ministry at Meadows. He recalled the closing remarks word for word like they were a prayer.

> "*To you young people in the congregation: when you are middle-aged or older and look back on what characterized Meadows Church during these precious times—Now!—it will seem like I stayed at Meadows for a long time, because it will have been for the entire span of your adolescence. To you older friends sitting out there this morning—parents, grandparents, others—I hope that you think that my time with you sped by, because time flies when . . . well when we're having . . . good times together. If I am so privileged to get this job, I hope my time with you will be enjoyable, and much, much more. Amen.*"

He was not experiencing the feelings he had hoped for and anticipated when he created "Leveling with you-out-there-in-the-pews . . . and God."

7

Charity

Toxic Charity

UNBEKNOWNST TO REV. EK or anyone else at Meadows, a little group of–they called themselves–Trouble Makers had formed. It included Paige, Jayne, Alan Mueller, Carleton Stark, and Keyshawn Gentry. Paige convened them in the wake of what she called Rev. Chris's hollow homily, ". . . that one he called leveling with us or something like that." Paige was inspired by a book she saw at home that her mother had bought but not yet read: *Toxic Charity* by a guy named Robert Lupton. It criticized the usual way that churches and secular non-profits try to help people. He offered new directions based on successes in Atlanta. Paige, like the others who had eagerly awaited what Chris would say in that sermon, was disappointed by what he didn't say. She had hoped that her pastor had read *Toxic Charity* and was going to share the message with the congregation.

It was no accident that the Trouble Makers met outside of church and without the pastor, the board, or representatives of the people in the pews. They–but especially Paige–were impatient and couldn't abide the premature criticism that would certainly push back at Lupton's ideas. He writes that unwittingly charities, including churches, often hurt those that they are try-ing to help. Much of the money or in-kind help is wasted by creating depen-dency and destroying personal initiative. He says that when we do for those in need what they have the capacity to do for themselves, we disempower them. This message struck a chord with Paige and the others.

The point is to team up with those you want to help, and let them help lead what you are doing, or be leaders themselves. Paige said, "After I read that book, I thought this stuff is for us. We can do it. The timing is right. The people are right, and we can get Pastor Chris to go along."

Mueller and Stark looked at each other with exaggerated frowns, heads tilted, palms up.

Paige's Sermon

Throughout his adult life as a parishioner and then as a clergyman, Chris had not liked the idea of special times that get the minister out of the pulpit in order to try something unusual like "Cannon Sunday," the week after Easter when–as the hackneyed story goes–you could fire a cannon in the sanctuary and nobody would be hit because so few were there. Or Holy Hilarity Sunday when (groan) comedy is tried. Or, a Sunday when anyone from the congregation who has a yen to get a sermon off his chest–it is almost always guys–would be given the green light and would strut their stuff, usually walking back and forth away from the pulpit.

Chris felt obligated to attend these gigs, but he gagged at the results. *"They make me nervous. Even threatened. Hey, I'm only being candid with myself."*

So, he surprised himself when he agreed to Paige's assertively presented idea of having the youth of the church lead a Sunday Service. She described it as an attempt to bring some "comic relief plus" to the congregation, a characterization that Chris first winced at. Upon reflection, he thought it would be welcomed, especially after the disappointment of his sermon when several key people expected him to say something about homelessness. So, he said go ahead and offered to help in any way.

"No," Paige said, "we can handle it. Please just relax and have faith, Pastor C."

The big day began with liturgy readings by members of the youth class sitting in a half-circle at the front of the sanctuary with her in the center. Members of Meadows sat on the edge of their pews in eager anticipation.

Read by Paige: "Job 8:21. He will once again fill your mouth with laughter and your lips with shouts of Joy."

From Pauline: "Prov 31:25-26. She is clothed with strength and dignity, and she laughs without fear of the future. When she speaks, her words are wise, and she gives instructions with kindness."

From Bruce: "Luke 6:21. Blessed are ye that hunger now: for ye shall be filled. Blessed are ye that weep now: for ye shall laugh."

From Beverly: "Prov 15:15 For the despondent, every day brings trouble; for the happy heart, life is a continual feast."

From Kenneth (in a hyper-dramatic voice): "1 Sam 5:9. The hand of the Lord was against the city with a very great destruction; and He smote the men of the city, both small and great, and they had hemorrhoids in their secret parts."

Nobody laughed. Paige interjected, "That was supposed to be funny," and everybody laughed. Then she took over, reading more passages herself.

"Prov 19:17 Whoever is generous to the poor lends to the Lord, and he will repay him for his deed.

"Matt 8:20 And Jesus said to him, "Foxes have holes, and birds of the air have nests, but the Son of Man has nowhere to lay his head."

"Matt 25:35 For I was hungry and you gave me food, I was thirsty and you gave me drink, I was a stranger and you welcomed me."

Paige then said, 'Whoa. I'm getting pretty serious here. This gig is supposed to be funny. Hilarious. (A few people in the congregation chuckled.). Let's move on. We youth of the church in planning this–let's call it a sermon–were partly inspired by Garrison Keillor, the guy who used to host A Prairie Home Companion on NPR before he was put out to pasture. Each year he would have a joke show, one where literally hundreds of supposedly funny passages or wise cracks were fired at the audiences listening to their radio or paying big bucks to sit in front of him, usually at the Fitzgerald Theater in St. Paul. So, let the show–the sermon–begin. She pointed at Gloria who read "Highest Number."

"Recently while we were eating lunch after church, my youngest son asked me what the highest number I had ever counted up to was. I said I didn't know. Then I asked him how high he has counted.

"5,372," came the prompt reply.

"Oh," I said. "Why did you stop there?"

"The sermon was over."

Lots of forced laughs and sweet smiles from the congregation as everyone looked over at Pastor Ek sitting front row left in the pews. Then Margaret read something she called "The Pearly Gates."

"A minister dies and is waiting in line at the Pearly Gates. Ahead of him is a guy who's dressed in sunglasses, a loud shirt, leather jacket, and jeans. Saint Peter addresses this guy: 'Who are you, so that I may know whether or not to admit you to the Kingdom of Heaven?' The guy replies: 'I'm Joe Cohen, taxi driver, of Noo Yawk City.' St. Peter consults his list, smiles, and says to the taxi driver, 'Take this silken robe and golden staff and enter the Kingdom of Heaven.'

"The taxi driver goes into Heaven with his robe and staff, and it's the minister's turn. He stands erect and booms out, 'I am Joseph Snow, pastor of my church for the last forty-three years.' St. Peter consults his list, and says to the minister, 'Take this cotton robe and wooden staff and enter the Kingdom of Heaven.'

"'Just a minute,' says the minister. 'That man was a taxi driver, and he gets a silken robe and golden staff. How can this be?'

"'Up here, we work by results,' says Saint Peter. 'While you preached, people slept; while he drove, people prayed.'"

Everyone laughed. Chris covered his head in mock shame. (He loved it.) Then Jimmy read: "The Dying Irish Nun."

"The wise old Mother Superior from County Tipperary was ready to enter the Kingdom of Heaven. The nuns gathered around her bed trying to make her comfortable. They gave her some warm milk to drink, but she refused it. Then one nun took the glass back to the kitchen. Remembering a bottle of Irish whiskey that they had received as a gift the previous Christmas, she opened and poured a generous amount into the warm milk.

"When she walked back to Mother Superior's bed, she held the glass to her lips. Mother drank a little, then a little more. Before they knew it, she had drunk the whole glass down to the last drop. 'Mother,' the nuns asked in earnest, 'please give us some wisdom before you die.'

"Slowly she raised up in bed and with a pious look on her face said, 'Don't sell that cow.'"

An explosion of guffaws, hoots, and hollers. They loved it. Then Ronnie read: "Thunderstorm."

"When a mother saw a thunderstorm forming in mid-afternoon, she worried about her seven-year-old daughter who would be walking three blocks home from school. Deciding to meet the child half way, the mother saw her walking nonchalantly along, stopping to smile whenever lightning flashed. Finally seeing her mother, the little girl ran to her, explaining enthusiastically, 'All the way home, God's been taking my picture!'"

The place filled with sweet smiles and 'awwwwhhhs. Then Mary read "Moses, Jesus, and an Old Bearded Man."

"These three were out playing golf one day. Moses sauntered up to the tee and smoked a big drive down the middle, but it hit something and rolled toward a water hole. Quickly he raised his club, the water parted, and the ball winked back at him from a perfect lie. He looked at the others, full of self-satisfaction.

"Next, Jesus hit a nice long one, but right toward the same hazard. It found the center and stayed there, gently floating. Jesus casually walked out on the water and pitched it up onto the green. A gimme putt. This Son of Man couldn't suppress a proud smile.

"The third guy gets up and sort of randomly whacks the ball with a funny swing. It heads over the fence into oncoming traffic on an adjacent street. It glances off a truck and hits a tree. From there it bounces onto the roof of a shack and rolls down into the gutter, out onto the fairway, and right toward the pond. On the way, it hits a little stone and bounces onto a lily pad where it rests quietly. Suddenly, a very large bullfrog jumps up on the lily pad and snatches the ball into his mouth. Just then, an eagle swoops down and grabs the frog and flies away. As they pass over the green, the frog squeals with fright and drops the ball, which bounces right into the cup for a beautiful hole in one. A miracle.

"Moses then turns to Jesus and says, 'I hate playing with your Dad. He's such a show off.'"

Groans. Big ones that wouldn't stop, followed by a scattering of tepid applause. But everyone was smiling. Paige thought, *"Corn eee."*

After a pause that let everyone calm down, she took over again and introduced a story she called "Jesus was a racist."

"Jesus was a racist," said the first person.

"What in the world are you talking about?" answered the next.

"He was. A subtle one. He didn't come right out and say it, but he didn't speak out against it either.

"Uh, what is the 'it?'"

"Slavery."

"What?"

"Well, all over in the New Testament there is talk of slavery, but Jesus doesn't speak out against it. He obviously either tolerates it or is afraid to bring it up. Jesus was a racist!"

Nobody laughed or applauded. The sanctuary had turned silent and only the honk of a horn outside could be heard. Then a voice from a back pew called out, "That's not funny." Paige nodded in agreement.

Then she read, "The Homeless Couple and the United Church of Christ Pastor." Pastor Ek squirmed.

"This man of god was driving to his church when he saw two people bending over in the grass. He decided to see why. He walked over to them and asked what they were doing. One of them said they were homeless and grass was the only thing they could eat. The pastor said, 'You can eat over at the church.'

"The woman said, 'But we have nine children. Will there be enough?'"

"'Oh yes,' pastor replied, 'the grass is 2 1/2 inches taller over there.'"

Nobody laughed or clapped or booed. Bruce plunged into the silence:

"Homeless people here are different." He self-consciously cleared his throat and repeated, "Homeless people *here* are different. Did you ever notice that? Our homeless people are serious, man. They have signs that not only say, 'Will work for food,' but some of them put in their orders: Baked potato, salad, shrimp, sweet potato pie, sour chives, prime rib."

There were a couple of half-hearted laughs that hit a stony wall of silence. Then Tommy raised his finger, and launched into a little story:

"I was walking down the street when I was accosted by a particularly dirty and shabby-looking homeless-looking man who asked me for a couple of dollars for dinner. I took out my wallet, extracted ten dollars and asked, 'If I give you this money, will you buy some beer with it instead of dinner?'

"'No, I had to stop drinking years ago,' the homeless man replied.

"'Will you use it to go fishing instead of buying food?' I asked.

"'No, I don't waste time fishing,' the homeless man said, 'I need to spend all my time trying to stay alive.'

"'Will you spend this on golf?' I asked.

"'Are you nuts?' replied the homeless man. 'I beat that addiction 20 years ago!'

"'Well,' I said, 'I'm not going to give you money. Instead, I'm going to take you home for a shower and a terrific dinner cooked by my wife.'

"The homeless man was astounded. 'Won't your wife be furious with you for doing that?'

"I replied, 'Don't worry. It's important for her to see what a man looks like after he has given up golf.'"

About half of the kids who were still up front laughed hard, as if on cue. The congregation followed, their voices growing into a wave of full-throated approval capped off by applause.

The rest of the youngsters had left the front during the story and taken seats in various parts of the sanctuary. As soon as things quieted down one of them, Beverly, stood up from a back pew, pointed her finger hither and yon and said, "I love you folks, all of you. I really do, so I don't want to offend you or betray my affection, but, *but* I'll bet you're so sophisticated and politically correct that you *wouldn't* laugh as hard or at all if women or African-Americans or Latinos were the butt of that joke. But, the homeless: they have so little advocacy and support, even in this church that claims to support Helping Hands. Right?" She panned her glance over her young pals who were nodding.

Inside, Beverly was seething. She had prepared her comments well in advance, but never did she anticipate the raw emotion that came with her shaking, powerful voice. She finished by asking, "How many of you would take a homeless person into your home? Come on. Raise your hands."

Stop Sign and Confluence did right away, followed by Ebby Stone. Joyce called out, "I don't know. I am humiliated to mention this, but I doubt if I would."

Jayne Nova said, "I wouldn't. Wouldn't take anyone into my house (she paused) except maybe Pastor Ek."

He blushed. Almost everyone–including Stop Sign and Confluence and the kids–laughed and applauded. Some went stone-faced and silent, but the awkward mood was broken, and Paige regained their attention by firmly whacking a mallet on a piece of wood, like a judge would do.

"Okay," she said. "Maybe the heart of our sermon is starting to beat." Then gazing toward the ceiling of the sanctuary she called out: "Do we miss the big picture because we see the needs of *our* organization–*our* church– first and foremost?"

And then she pointed to Ronnie who said, "Whenever there is sustained one-way giving, unwholesome dynamics and pathologies fester under the cover of kindheartedness." He nodded to Gloria who said,

"Many churches want their members to feel good about serving the poor, but no one really wants to become involved in messy relationships." She pointed her finger at Pauline, who said,

"To the extent that the homeless are enabled to participate in the systems intended to serve them, their worth is enhanced."

At this point Mrs. Snyder stood up, waited for the congregation to give her their full attention, and said, "What in the 'H' is going on here? Is this a church or a madhouse? Pastor Ek, did you know this was going to happen? Did you help them plan it?"

Before he could answer Louise Almain stood up and said, with a tone that was overly solicitous, "Whoa, Mrs. S. Isn't this a service that you will remember for a long time? We have witnessed something that will keep us talking and thinking."

Ebby Stone popped up and added, "Look, I came to church this morning expecting to be lectured to by this kid–pointing at Paige–and dreading every moment of it, but isn't she–aren't they–*right*?"

"Hmmm. I could live with that," Paige said so everyone could hear.

Then she motioned to the organist to play the hymn *Children of the Heavenly Father* softly in the background.

Finally, in a gesture intended to return them to the real world, Paige indicated that there would be no time of sharing Joys and Concerns. She said that "we children" will be at the back of the church to shake your hands, or whatever. She motioned for the organ to reprise the hymn as a quiet postlude while she recited a benediction from Rom 15:5-6.

"May the God of endurance and encouragement grant you to live in such harmony with one another, in accord with Christ Jesus, that together you may with one voice glorify the God and Father of our Lord Jesus Christ."

Few congregants went through the reception line. Most of them said something like "good job" without elaboration as they quickly marched by. Paige received a letter the next day, which bothered her for a bit, but made her smile at the end. It said, "There is little of Christ in this church. The place is too social. The old people around here are being ignored. I did like the way you stuck to traditional music, however: no guitars or castanets or bells." It closed by saying, "I think you are the real pastor of this church, which I am leaving, hopefully temporarily. Not because of you, though. The leaving."

Another Path

Pastor Chris had thought about nothing but Paige's sermon and service during the early part of the week leading up to the monthly Wednesday meeting of local pastors. He had cancelled his usual Monday golf game with Jayne, and the socializing that accompanied it. Lately, they were connecting, but he just wasn't up to it this time. Chris's agonizing conclusion was that Paige is a better preacher then he is. He hated admitting it, but received consolation by acknowledging that he was being candid and honest. In Chicago, he once crossed paths with a kid that everyone called a natural pastor, better than Chris was or perhaps ever would be. Paige now fell into that category although he acknowledged that he would not like to have her as his daughter. Poor Joyce.

On the Wednesday, Pastor Chris attended this meeting that he always looked forward to: a gathering of local ministers. He usually kept quiet while others went on, but today when the agenda's "questions for the good of the body" came up, Chris asked the group of about fifteen, "How do you deal with the matter of homeless people who cross our paths? We all meet them, yes?" Nobody gave an answer right away, and the mood morphed into one of those nervous times when somebody should say something.

Finally, Pastor Jones broke the tension: "I send them to the local social service office."

Another awkward silence.

Then the new minister from the Baptist church near the campus said, "But Chris, why do you ask? I thought you liberal UCCers had this matter all wrapped up. I hate to admit it but I wish we had the reputation you people do regarding Helping Hands. Do you have doubts, oh Christian Brother?"

Nervous sounding laughter from everyone didn't quite break the tension. Then the priest from the local Episcopalian congregation said, "You know, Pastor Ek, a lot of us are envious or downright jealous of what you do over there at Fair Are the Meadows or what some of us call That Country Club Congregation that you lead. By the way, do they cover the costs for all that golf you play on Monday mornings and beyond?"

Laughter flowed so spontaneously that it made Chris feel at home and brought him back to the earlier question about homelessness. He thought, *"Should I tell them what Paige is doing?"* And he tucked away in his memory folder those words that didn't sound as bad as they used to: Country Club Congregation.

Before he could say anything, another pastor spoke up head down. "We don't do socially active stuff. We don't do things that secular society is paid to do. I've had homeless people come to our place and I just tell them to go to (he named a place Chris had never heard of.). I tell them it's not our thing, but we would love to have them in our pews on Sunday, however they dress and however they smell. I get a kick out of telling them that and sometimes they laugh with me."

Chris couldn't imagine Meadows taking a stance like that church, but he had to admit to himself that it would be sweet just preaching and not having to be all things to all people. *"How is that possible,"* he mused, *"to do it well? Maybe I'm not a liberal Congregationalist after all. Or a minister."*

Chris left the meeting with more questions than answers but with one little resolution: *"No golf for me for, well, a week or two."*

8

Don't Hold Back

Paige & Sharon

DURING THESE DAYS PAIGE was in the early stages of a budding friendship
with Sharon. They met as students in a class at Belle Waters Memorial High
School called Creating Things and Ideas, a team-taught interdisciplinary
offering that encouraged students to become–according to the course description–imaginative, daring, and practical. At the beginning of the first
gathering, Paige leaned over to the girl sitting next to her:

"Hi, I'm Paige."

"Hi, I'm Sharon," and rather formally Sharon reached out to shake
Paige's hand. They held on to each other for a long time as Paige held back
a smile. She later acknowledged that this little bonding was the first signal
that Sharon was somebody she would like to know better. Somebody who
seemed to like her.

That first day kids were instructed to pair up with someone that they
didn't know in order to participate in something called "Don't Hold back!"
an exercise in creative thinking designed to develop a large pool of ideas that
might turn out to be useful in addressing a challenge. The teacher asked for
examples that they could work on. Sharon suggested the problem of providing–what she called–home bases for people. Places where they can be safe
and thoughtful. More than one kid rolled their eyes, but the teacher cleared
her throat and said, with a wink and smile, "No criticism, please. We'll have
time for that later." Paige liked what was happening. She and Sharon looked
at each other, nodded, and were in the earliest stage of becoming a pair.

"Don't Hold Back"

Ground Rules

The more ideas you come up with, the better.

The wilder they may seem, the better.

Build and combine your ideas onto those of your partner's.

And for now: no idea squelching. No criticism of ideas that others present or no holding back of your own. Turn them loose! Don't hold back.

Students' ideas

"Cardboard boxes."

"Cars in junkyards."

"Cars anywhere."

"Caves."

"Nests, especially Baltimore oriole ones."

"Deserted houses. There are quite a few in Belle Waters."

"Unused rooms in anyone's house, like a guest room."

"Unused rooms in churches. Ours has lots of them."

"Make safety spaces for kids in schools."

"Ice caves, or dugout areas in hills."

"Big golf bags."

"Thick hedges. Like carved out areas. Mazes."

"A church. Their big room. What's it called? The nave?"

"Underneath places: beds, basements, those where auto repair shops change oil."

"A secret spot on a golf course."

"A hut, like you find on some golf courses where they sell refreshments."

"A motorized golf cart, one with plastic around it to keep out the rain."

"Unused places in golf clubhouses."

"My home," Paige said. Sharon looked at her. Paige shrugged and smiled. Then Paige said, "Send them to Rockford. Zion Lutheran on Sixth Street."

Paige had few close friends. None, really. She didn't dislike her peers and when they got to know her, they usually respected her intelligence and vigor. Beyond her hearing they referred to her as "a true individual, somebody marching to a different drummer," innocuous labels, but sometimes the critiques had a bite: "*Paige is smart and she thinks she's smart, but in some ways, she is really stupid. Like in–what do they call it–social intelligence? She doesn't know how to approach people or listen to them.*"

Up to this point nobody had cultivated her as a close chum. Nor had she them. To herself she assumed that everyone thought she was stuck up and snooty. She once overheard someone say she seemed more comfortable with adults. She didn't care–"*Maybe I am*," she told herself–but privately she longed to be part of a devoted friendship like the ones she observed at church and school.

Then came Sharon: a fascinating female and just maybe a kindred spirit. As time went by, Paige saw impressive intelligence in the girl: Her awareness of subtle themes in music when they went to concerts and recitals around town. Her sharp eye for variations in budding plants as they strolled through a nearby nature park. Her performance in class. Her appreciation for the mechanics of a sound golf swing as they talked about the game that was pulling Paige in, although as far as Paige could tell, Sharon didn't play the game.

She would ask questions about golf that Paige couldn't readily answer: Why are most players right-handed? Why is it considered a game for the rich? Who is Moe Norman–he's somebody I'd like to learn more about? Paige wasn't used to getting queries from her peers that she couldn't answer. She interpreted them as interrogations, but it was different with Sharon. Paige liked being challenged by this curious friend who was her intellectual equal.

And she looked so natural, Sharon did. She wasn't trying to impress anyone with affectations or trendy clothes. When Paige realized this, she felt a tang of guilt. Her own hair had those streaks of purple highlights, and she squinted into the mirror every morning to put on a little eye liner and mascara. Her finger- and toenails got a new coat of polish at least once a week. She searched consignment stores for used, fashionable jeans and baggy sweatshirts that had just the right amount of wear. Not obviously pre-ripped. Paige tried to portray a natural look that would be acceptable to her school peers.

Sharon had it.

Later in the week when she met Sharon, Paige was uncharacteristically quiet and listening as some of her church friends complimented her mother. One of them said, "Mrs. Ahlgren always looks so good–so right–but I'll bet she doesn't work at it. My mother spends so much time getting her face ready in the morning, and she sometimes changes clothes twice before going out. Bet your mom doesn't do that, does she, Paige?" Paige nodded and smiled. She was thinking about Sharon, another natural whose clothes were worn just right.

Sharon shared Paige's tendency to quickly criticize anything and anybody, but she was quiet about it. A little thumbs up or smile from Sharon when Paige shot from the hip told Paige that her friend was on her side. Somebody she could trust. Paige also saw wariness in Sharon. Like she was looking over her shoulder for someone or something. When they would go to the cafeteria, Sharon never wanted to have her back to the door. Paige didn't say anything about it, but thought, "*I like that quality. She's alert and aware. Attentive to details that others often miss. No pushover.*" Paige thought of herself that way: no pushover. More than once these days she mused, "*Our Pastor Chris. He's a pushover. A sweet man, but easy to manipulate.*"

Paige looked forward to being with Sharon and the feeling was mutual. The more they realized they had similar interests and values, the more time they spent together. When they coincidentally met while changing classes or at lunch, they hugged, something Paige never did before. Part of Paige's attraction to Sharon was the girl's–well–mystery. She didn't talk at all about her family or her past, but she seemed so street smart, aware and savvy. Paige noticed this in Sharon's clothes: not aimed at impressing anybody but trendy and well worn; stylish in a personalized, scruffy way that worked, but Sharon didn't seem interested in showing off. She could never be considered a conspicuous consumer. And she had a natural way with others. Paige called it poise.

Something Clicked

Chris went eleven days without playing golf. He thought about the game on and off, but his serious preoccupations kept drifting to Jayne. He missed playing a round with her as usual on the Monday, and while preparing the Sunday sermon, a passage from *Gilead* by Marilynne Robinson flashed into his head–the one where pastor John Ames looks out into the upturned faces of the seated parishioners and with tingles in body and soul, sees fully for the first time the woman who would become his wife. Chris shook his head vigorously side to side, smiled, and said to himself. "*Please don't go there.*" But he had.

During the days away from the golf course, without him touching a club, Chris's dormant swing had settled into a useful groove all on its own. Like the results of gravity and jostling that move awkwardly stuffed things around in our luggage during a journey and makes everything look packed better when we open it at our destination, everything worked when Chris got back out on the links Friday morning. Playing alone he accomplished something he had only dreamed of: He broke eighty for the first time. With a seventy-four! He could hardly believe it. This score was so far beyond his usual fantasy best-case scenario that he thought of it in the same category as that hole in one in Florida: manna from somewhere. He was in possession of a fully functioning golf swing.

Par on the first nine at Muni Golf Course in Belle Waters goes 444 345 444 for a 36: At the break Chris's card read: 744 535 545 for a 42. Three under an average of fives per hole, a way of keeping track of how he's doing that is more reasonable than comparing himself against the high bar of par. Not bad, but his back nine made a statement like something out of a Michael Murphy novel. Par there is 534 434 434 for a 34. Chris went 622 535 423 for 32. A two under par–thirteen under fives–thirty-two! With three 2's! And with three bogies! Giving him a seventy-four! Sixteen under fives on nine holes! Thanks be to the Lord! May miracles never cease!

Back home Chris did what every captive golfer does. He analyzed his play hole by hole. *"The first hole on each nine killed me. I was four over on those alone. I could have had a seventy with pars there. Wow."* Utilizing this type of cherry picking, Chris didn't acknowledge the against-the-odds spewing of good fortune that had him holing out from off the green three times for the seventy-four: that birdie with a chip-in on number five, that full eight-iron eagle on number twelve, and for that bogie pitch that went in on number fifteen. Over the years when he reflected back on this round, he acknowledged that had the Lord not been helping him out that day, he could have wound up in the low eighties rather than the mid-seventies. Well below ninety and totally respectable. But the Lord did help him. That day. Or maybe the Lord had nothing to do with it.

His next time out with Jayne the following Monday, after having jabbered on and on about how he had found his game with the 74, found him scoring 866 266 665 for a 51 on the front nine followed by 573 845 666 for a 50 on the back total. One hundred one for the eighteen. She had a 78 that could have been much better had her putting been on and her gimpy right shoulder at 100%. She usually carried the bag on her right shoulder, like Chris, but used a pull cart this day.

Even with her temporary physical handicap, Jayne regularly outdrove Chris. She was lithe and tan and strong and fit. Powerful like Olympic female athletes who don't have muscles that bulge. Her swing was smooth and simple with great club head speed entering the hitting the area. Stunning. The swing. The scene. Jayne.

By hole number three she was teasing the Rev. Ek mercilessly. As an experienced golfer, she realized that anyone who had had a fine round one day could start out bad the next time out, so she kept quiet as she wrote down that quadruple bogie 8 for him on the first hole. But after his–she called them goofy–swings on the next two holes that produced a brace of double bogies following the quad, she couldn't keep her big mouth shut. She fired away like a kid with a water rifle full of grapefruit juice.

"Uh, where did that grooved swing–that you've been bragging about– go? Did God reach down and take it back? Professor Keyshawn Gentry would spank you if he saw your bodily contortions today. Hmmm, let's see: So far, you're eight over par for three holes. Just who was your scorekeeper that day when your numbers took a dizzying dive? Whoops, you said you were playing alone. Could there have been some–hmmm–pencil pushing? Or fantasy scoring? Wish fulfillment brought to life in the freedom of your solitude? Fiction!?"

This teasing critique hovered close to affection, but without any smiles or winks. Justifiable and tangy. He had lost the swing that brought his miracle seventy-four, and her ostensibly cruel comments would sound hurtful to a person overhearing her, but there was something about them–the comments and her tone–that sped up his heart. He remembered what he had preached in a recent sermon: "*We kid people we like. How they receive it is a little test in reciprocity and friendship.*"

His soaring six iron to eight feet on number four and the left-to-right downhill putt that dove in for a birdie deuce quieted her down, and he couldn't resist saying, foolishly, "I'm back!"

She flashed that gorgeous smile, brushed knuckles with him and wrote down the 2, but thought "*We'll see if he's really back.*" She didn't have to wait long. Four sixes in a row–seven over par on that stretch–had him at six over fives for the eight holes played. A respectable bogie on the tough number nine gave him that 51. Jayne knew that the same golfer who shoots a 42 a side one day can easily take 51 strokes the next time out, but she couldn't resist having at him again, especially since Chis seemed to be pouting. "Has my baby's birthday balloon burst? Was that 74 a dream that faded at the break of day? Isn't there a hymn that puts us into our places? Let's sing the key verse together . . . C'mon."

She bumped her hip against his and in a pure alto voice quietly crooned a verse from, *Our God, Our Help in Ages Past* by Isaac Watts.

> Time, like an ever-rolling stream,
> Bears all of us away;
> We fly forgotten, as a dream
> Dies at the opening day . . .

And then she said, "So does that magic golf swing die, that one that comes out of the blue and teases and kisses us before going all fickle."

Of course, Chris knew the verse from the hymn, and got all emotional as the melody ran through his head. He frowned for a few more seconds, then laughed out loud. He was ready when Jayne started singing it again, and joined her with the energy of a minister garbed in his Sunday regalia feeling fulfilled after hitting all the key points in a sermon and then harmonizing with the choir.

Jayne said, "Let's do it one last time," and they did, slowly harmonizing. Then he wrapped his arms around her, and they bent into a pose like that military guy and his new-found gal pictured in all the newspapers on VE day at the end of WWII, and kissed long and sweet and wet and deep. Right there on the golf course. When they were done, Jayne faked a scowl and said, "We're all tied up in knots, like your swing."

After hitting their tee shots on the tenth hole they walked down the fairway hand in hand, she pulling the trolley on her left, he with his clubs over his right shoulder. He parred it, but then screwed up royally taking seven on the par 3 eleventh. Chris went silent once more. Finally, with scorecard and pencil at the ready, Jayne cleared her throat and asked him what the bad news was for the hole—even though she knew. He raised his hands like Jesus on the cross and called out for the world to hear: "A seven! I hit the ball seven times on that par three. I did it. I'm totally accountable for it. I have nobody to blame but myself! Write it down, woman!"

His head was whirling. He thought of the passage from *Golf in the Kingdom* where Michael Murphy, while trying hard to impress Shivas Irons, floundered big time on the first nine at what had to be the Old Course at St. Andrews, but is called Burning Bush. Murphy in brutal confession writes, "I leaned back and looked at the sky, then raised my arm to God and gave Him the finger." Now here at the Belle Waters Municipal golf course—everyone calls it Muni—while trying hard to impress Jayne Nova, Chris Ek didn't do what Michael Murphy did, but it came to his mind, and isn't that about the same? He looked over at Jayne. She was so limber gliding along, like a cat on a mission.

On the next tee after she smacked a drive down the middle 240 yards, he started to tell her—for the umpteenth time—about the eagle he had on this hole during his 74, but she said, "Shut up and play, boy." He felt a tingle down low as he smoked a power fade 260 yards that left him with a wedge to the green. He almost sank this one—it danced around the flagstick—and stroked his three-footer into the center of the hole for a birdie. He was tempted to stick out his chest and say *"three under on this rascal for the last two times out"* but kept it to himself. Best that he did considering the snowman on number thirteen for his third quadruple bogie of the round. Jayne ratcheted up the mocking following each of his errant shots, finally going after him with her club as a rapier. Poke. Poke. Poke.

She said, "Think, Pastor Ek. What would Professor Keyshawn Gentry tell you to do in times like these?"

Chris thought a little bit, but his main preoccupation was not on past golfing triumphs. This round and day and playing partner were better than any old seventy-four.

Rather than just dropping Chris off and going on her way in the Miata, Jayne came inside. He hadn't invited her, even though he later realized that he should have. Holding his hand, she led him from the car to the garage, where he dropped off his clubs, and then to the side entrance. Now fully alert, he held the door open with his chin up high followed by a little bow from the waist like a butler greeting visiting aristocracy. They got to know each other up close that morning, Jayne and Chris. He rubbed her bad shoulder and they, well, let's say they shared sweet treats. Before she left he let her know that he appreciated her friendship in addition to–he called it–our little tastes of heaven.

Then he said, "It's not easy for a single minister to connect–or whatever–within a faith community. If someone you could get together with is in the congregation there's a likelihood for jealousy on the part of others. And certainly gossip."

She had been studying him with that mock frown. "What do you mean 'whatever'?"

"Duh, my dear, what do you think?" He faked stammering with a silly little grin on his face.

She poked him in the ribs with her finger and then started tickling him. "C'mon. Tell me. Say it. Be candid like you said we should be. You said that from the pulpit. Say it!"

"Well, let's face it. We are more than friends."

She paused and looked out the window for what he thought was an eternity. Then she nibbled on his ear and whispered, "So just what are we?"

On the drive back to her house she mused out loud about how Chris gathers sermon topics from his golfing adventures. "*I do too from mine–for my lectures–especially those about manipulative games that people play.*" During her very next class period a student asked if she ever does that sort of thing.

"Of course," she said.

Zion

On Thursday at 7:45 a.m. Paige, Sharon, and Jayne met in front of Fair
Are the Meadows Church. A rusty 1992 white Dodge Caravan pulled up a
minute later with Carleton in the driver's seat and Alan riding shotgun. It
smelled of cigarettes and there was so much dirt and debris on the floor that
Alan said they could grow weed "right in here!" Everyone laughed. Spirits
were high. They were about to go to Rockford and take a tour of Zion Lutheran Church, a sanctuary and campus that spoke not just its two historical
languages–Swedish and English–but two more as well. Laotian and Spanish.

Paige summarized the impact of Zion: "It's a church that acted on its
commitment and took a risk. They led the broader community. The ob-
stacles and prejudices were–and continue to be–enormous, but Zion has
stuck to it and the seeds sown by their efforts are bearing fruit to this day
as new versions of old challenges hang on. Don't get me wrong. There is a
long way to go."

Welcoming new Americans from the surrounding households into
the congregation was one goal of senior pastor Denver Bitner and a core
of dedicated members; another was to rehabilitate the neighborhood. The
area around Zion's location at Fifth Avenue and Sixth Street had slid from
neat well-maintained homes of Swedish-American immigrants and their
descendants beginning in the last third of the nineteenth century and extending to the 1960s to a mixture of abused and vacant buildings. Too many
of them crack houses. A safe vigorous neighborhood had descended into a
crime-infested deteriorating one starting in the troubled late 1970s. In the
middle of it was a precious oasis: Zion. A core of Good Samaritans, led by
Pastor Bitner, hung on to help navigate a road to recovery.

Paige had visited Zion before, and she knew where she wanted to go as
she instructed Carleton to drive around so they could get a feel for this part
of town before meeting Pastor Bitner. She took them south on Sixth Street
past a procession of Lutheran churches once full of Swedish-Americans of
all ages. There was Emanuel on Third Avenue, Zion on Fifth Avenue, and
Salem on Sixteenth Avenue. They turned east on Eighteenth Avenue before
heading back north on Eighth Street–past a former hotel that became a flop-
house before Zion's Development Corporation had turned it into a refuge
for the homeless.

Denver Bitner had grown up in the neighborhood. After college and
seminary, he returned to serve as youth director at Zion before moving into
the senior pastor's role. His energy, knowledge, and devotion to the cause
ultimately allowed Zion to dream big dreams, and turn them into reality,
but it wasn't easy. It isn't easy.

Bitner was waiting for the Belle Waterers at the Zion-inspired eatery called Katie's Cup located in the old Lantow's pharmacy site on the southeast corner of Fourth Avenue and Seventh Street. He described it as a fabulous coffee and lunch shop that has become a gathering hub for the neighborhood and a birthplace for ideas. After handshakes and a hug from Paige, he gave a brief history of Zion including what he called its fragile successes and still-festering challenges. He said that Rockford had one of the highest unemployment rates in the country starting in the late 1970s and that the neighborhood around Zion–and extending down Seventh Street to Broadway–was at its geographical center. While many resident Laotians, Latinos, African-Americans and others had struggled to survive and improve their lot, the area as well as the congregation needed help. Prostitution was thriving on Seventh Street and Broadway. Drug traffickers walked the streets openly. Gun violence grew to such an extent that Rockford–led by this area–was on a short-list of the most violent communities in the United States. And there was a malignancy of homelessness.

Then he took them on a walking tour. They first stopped in at Patriots' Gateway, a large multi-purpose building to the west of the church that has a gymnasium, classrooms, and offices, and operates as a school. Just to the south was the "golf course"–a practice area for kids with tee boxes, greens, and a routing of holes. Carleton and Al stood mouths agape. Jayne's mind was processing. Paige had kept this as a surprise for her Belle Waters compatriots.

She said, "Look! A golf facility in the midst of high-density urban challenges. It came out of the energy that accompanied two Tiger Woods Clinics sponsored by Rockford and Belle Waters during the early 2000's."

They walked past renovated homes and community-maintained gardens before stopping by the Sixth Street railway station that was end of the line for Swedish immigrants coming to Rockford long ago. Then they got into Zion's van and went to that adjacent Rockford problem area: Broadway. As recently as the late 1960s neat little shops, a Swedish bakery, and furniture stores brought all of Rockford to this Southeast side neighborhood and retail center. There was a big celebration on Broadway when Sweden's Ingemar Johansson won the World's Heavyweight Boxing title in 1959. Like the earlier Seventh Street shopping center near Zion, Broadway reached a peak of family friendly Americana in these years and then sank, scraping bottom during the late 1970s economic implosion. In the years to follow, homelessness, drugs, and prostitution painted its face. As former Rockfordians returned to town and drove past this neighborhood of their childhood, tears washed over smiles.

While they slowly motored along, Bitner described the Zion Development Corporation (ZDC). It was founded in 1982 to address economic needs of the neighborhood, which by then had become part of the larger near east side of Rockford called MidTown. Activities of ZDC in the 1980s include collaboration with industries to provide jobs, offering English as a Second Language classes through Rock Valley College, purchasing houses for rehabilitation, and opening a textile art facility to enable Hmong residents to sell their work on consignment. ZDC purchased and operated Top Hat Catering & Wedding Center and Oriental Express Restaurant on Broadway. Sopha Electronics came to Seventh Street with ZDC's help, which partnered in opening "The Dove," an employment training and business start-up opportunity for military veterans learning fiberglass technology.

In the 1990s ZDC purchased and rehabilitated apartment buildings in the 500 block of Fifth Street and provided leadership in the formation of the Seventh Street Area Development Council, forerunner of MidTown District. They built twelve new energy-efficient town homes, the first new residential construction in the neighborhood in decades. They completed a $1 million renovation of the National Building on Seventh Street, transforming a deteriorated, dangerous structure into safe, decent, affordable apartment and commercial space.

In the 2000s ZDC transformed the diminished Grand Hotel on Broadway into apartments, which became Rockford's first permanent facility for homeless people, a $5.3 million-dollar project. It had previously been designated as the most dangerous building in nine counties according to police records. And the list went on. ZDC financed these efforts via private donations, fund-raisers, and grants from foundations and governmental organizations. And sweat equity.

As soon as they packed into the Caravan for the ride back to Belle Waters, Paige said to nobody in particular, "Well, what do you think? Do you get any ideas for Belle Waters? For Meadows? Or, Carleton, for golf course design, you architect, you?"

Jayne jumped in, "Hey, Carleton. That golf spot at Zion reminded me of something you could do at Meadows. Inside the place. Using the acres of space in Pastor Chris's office. Our church needs a putting green, surrounded by hazards, of course."

Sharon hadn't said anything on the ride back to Wisconsin, but she looked deep in thought.

"I'm Not Who You Think"

Carleton dropped off the three women in front of Fair Are the Meadows. Jayne headed north on foot across campus to her office. Paige and Sharon moseyed eastwardly to the college Poetry Garden, where they sat side by side on a bench. They hadn't spoken since getting out of the van, and they hadn't planned to wind up here.

Sharon's soft words broke what Paige later described as their trance. Eyes filling with tears, Sharon looked long and hard at her friend. In a quavering voice she finally said, "I've got something to tell you. I'm not who you think. I'm homeless."

Paige froze, and she got dizzy. A few days before she had wondered about Sharon's personal circumstances, but the thoughts came and went. Now she could have taken Sharon's hands or given her a kiss. Instead they turned and stared straight ahead in one of those moments you never forget. Finally, Sharon wiped her face with her sleeve, and started talking. "I've wanted to tell you this for a while, but I just couldn't take the leap. I almost did on Monday. After school, I had a scene with Mr. B . . ."

"Your favorite teacher."

"Yeah. He asked me to see him. I didn't think much of it at the time, certainly nothing bad. I like being in school, even staying after. He started right out by saying, 'I notice your grades are slipping.' My heart sank. Doing well in school means so much to me. You know, it's that way with a lot of us homeless kids. We value our time in school and want to do well, and at the same time we don't want teachers or anyone to know that we are homeless. Mr. B was just being a conscientious guy when he brought up the grades. I bet he keeps his eyes on the grade point averages of lots of kids. Probably all of them, us. But when he said that to me, I lost it. I started crying and couldn't stop. You know, quiet weeping with shaking shoulders that goes on forever. Well, Mr. B didn't do what a lot of people would, like put his arm around me and say 'there, there', he just sat and listened. But I kept sobbing and shaking. He had touched something so profound in me, and it came to the surface. Finally, in a whisper he said, 'What is wrong, Sharon? This thing with the grades is not a big deal. I'm just giving you a little warning. You are a fine student. I want you to know that I care.'

"Well, I guess I knew that he cared. He always impressed me as a fine human being, but I knew he didn't know that I was homeless, so I did something that I hardly ever do. I got up and left. Usually, I don't run away from situations, but I had to be alone for a while.

"The next morning, I sought him out and said I had to share something personal. I quietly told him that I am homeless and school means everything to me and that I'm terrified of wasting my opportunity in high school if my grades are going down. Well, he listened again as I told him something about my background. Paige, you are listening now. I so appreciate it. Let me say this. Like many–most–homeless persons, I battle loneliness, stress, and anxiety. All of the time. Well, not actually all of the time. The hours in school are good, but the other times are scary. I feel so vulnerable and alone. It is very difficult for me to say this to you. Do you understand that? I really appreciate your just listening, Paige."

Sharon continued. "So, I told Mr. B some of the highlights–low lights?– of my life and he listened. And tears came from *his* eyes. He heard me. He is a person who helps all kids, but I wanted him to know my circumstances, and I'm glad I told him. You see, even Mr. B had a blind spot or a lack of awareness of what goes on in the lives of some of his students. Like me. But I know he heard what I was saying. He is a friend of people like me, or can be. Well, when he wiped his eyes and we started talking back and forth he said he had always assumed that I was stable and sound. From what some might call a good family. He didn't fully realize that homeless kids can be very good students. Among the best. He admitted –well, he said–that scales are falling from his eyes. He used those very words and went on to say that he had stereotypes of homeless kids, and that I didn't seem like one. I said we come in all varieties, and Mr. B and I smiled together. He had shared his vulnerability with me and I greatly appreciated it.

"Mr. B and I had to get to our classes. He had looked at his watch a couple of times. Finally, he said, 'This is very personal for you, isn't it, Sharon?' I held back my emotions and nodded. Paige, you are just the second person I have talked with about this. Have you ever heard of Project 16:49?"

"A little bit, maybe."

"Well, it's for those like me. I'm a 16:49er. Homeless. Can you believe it? Sixteen hours and 49 minutes is the amount of time between getting out of school at the end of one day and starting back the next morning. All too often it's the worst of times–longer during the weekends–and it's not when I feel good about myself if ever. Or feel good about anything. I certainly don't want to be thought of as homeless. The stereotypes and mistruths are endless: We're worthless . . . violent . . . drug infested . . . poor . . . hopeless . . . drunk. Now that is not all false. Some of them–us–are like that sometimes and others may be most of the time, but I'm sure not and neither are most of us. I think of myself as a serious student, and when Mr. B said those words, I immediately thought he must have found out about my homelessness, and was seeing me as one of them and patronizing me. Putting me in a box. Diminishing my potential. But it wasn't that at all. He was treating me as a normal good student. His tears came when he realized my situation and when he realized that he hadn't fully appreciated kids like me. That's what I think, anyway."

Sharon continued, "Do you know how many kids are homeless in the United States?" Paige took it as a rhetorical question and didn't react. "Well, hundreds of thousands at least, and I'm told that 40% of about three million homeless in the good old U.S. of A. are under seventeen years. So, I have company, but that's not a group that I want to be a part of. It scares me so much of the time, but school, and Mr. B, and you, Paige, have become bright parts of my, what is it? 24:00 minus 16:49 equals six hours and eleven minutes each weekday. [Paige had reflexively calculated it as *seven* hours and eleven minutes but decided to stay quiet.] And the scene in Rockford this morning moved me. For all practical purposes Rev. Bitner was talking about me when he brought up the pain and hurt that can hit any family, but that hits the homeless person harder. Somebody like me. I got kicked out. They wouldn't have me anymore . . ."

Paige's head was still whirling. Sharon went on.

"You know I was actually a caregiver at home. I looked after my grandparents who own the place–it's not the tidy house it used to be–and I guess I offended my slovenly mom and her drug-infested boyfriend who also live there. I think they felt guilty that I was doing what they should have. I didn't mind it. Cleaning up and doing chores. I liked it. Now I feel guilty that I am not with them–any of them–but I got into a humongous fight with my mom. I said, 'I'm leaving,' but didn't mean it. She said, 'Good. Go.' And I did. A battle of wills with everyone losers."

Paige spoke up. "So where do you stay at night? I guess I've never seen your home, or the absence of your home." Sharon smiled anemically.

"Well, sometimes with my half-sister and her kids. Sometimes with an older lady my grandparents know, but she has so much trouble and so little room. I have stayed in cars. I can see how people become hoarders: you need stuff to survive and a car has some space after you allow for a driver. I notice cars that are full to overflowing with–I never call it junk–it's, well I don't have a name for it, but it's really household furnishings. There's one that parks on a street next to the college–a car like that."

Paige said, "So this homeless bit has to be on your mind all the time. I'll bet you have lots of stories to . . ."

Sharon didn't let her finish, ". . . yes, let me tell you what happened just yesterday. I was with some kids in my AP biology class. We were dissecting fetal pigs, and we got silly. Talking about our toes as piggies, bringing up pigs from children's literature. Do you remember Piggling Bland from one of the Beatrice Potter books? My grandma gave me lots of those books when I was young. Well, anyway, somebody said these guys–meaning the little pink cadavers before us–should have been rescued, and he added, 'I would have taken one in.'

"Well, my heart sank as it does in times like that. Do you realize how often people speak of giving a so-called good home to animals? Lots. Always affectionately. Usually with a prideful tone for a job well done for those 'rescued.' I kept quiet at the start of the fetal pig adoption scene, but then something happened that put me over the top. Another guy said he likes the photographs you see in advertisements about adopting cats or dogs from animal rescue centers. He said the names and pictures slay him. He started rattling them off: Fifi, Pluto, Fido, Clark, Emily, Flat-face, Push-face (like for Persian cats) and on and on. Others joined in telling or making up names that they saw or would like to see in the advertisements: Baby doll, Cutesey Pie, Madonna, Woody Allen, Bill Murray, Fuzzy, Whiskers, Shit Face, Poop bottom, Puddin'–they were going on like they never would stop.

"Then one kid that I kinda liked, a guy named Lou, got all excited and pointed at me. 'I saw a photo of a dog they called Sharon!' Everyone looked at me and laughed. I was shocked beyond words. They came out of the blue–the example and my reaction. I burst into tears and ran from the room. I haven't seen any of those kids since, but I know that that incident, along with our Rockford trip, is behind my coming out to you now."

It looked like Sharon was ready to get up and leave. Paige stayed quiet. In spite of desperately wanting to share some comforting words, they didn't come, and it wouldn't have felt right. Instead she hugged Sharon, and they walked off together hand in hand past the college Anthropology Museum before Sharon squeezed her hard, broke away, and headed towards the student union.

As Paige walked home she reflected on a conversation she had with Pastor Chris recently surrounding the death of an old member of Meadows. Joyce Ahlgren had thought it would be nice if Paige went along with her to the funeral service, so she reluctantly did. Before joining a receiving line to console the mourners, Paige cornered Chris and asked him what she should say to them. He said you don't need to say anything. Just being here is a message that they will appreciate. Paige felt better about how she had reacted toward Sharon. Listening, but she couldn't help bringing the matter back to herself. "I think she likes me. I really do."

Don't Hold Back!

Later that evening Paige did something unusual. She confided in her mother. She told Mrs. Ahlgren all about Sharon. Their class together at school.

Their developing closeness. Sharon's big secret. Paige talked on and on and moved into the matter of Fair Are the Meadows United Church of Christ and what she called its "tepid reaction to homelessness." She told about the Trouble Makers group, her reaction to Chris's sermons, the homeless golfing guys, and her own growing obsession with homelessness. Then she said, "What should I do, Mom? What do you suggest? Could Sharon come and live with us?"

Joyce Ahlgren stayed quiet. Then she said, "Let me think about it." Joyce had a very different take on the church's participation with Helping Hands. She thought it was a big help to homeless people, and to the congregation.

After a restless night, Joyce went swimming at her health club early the next morning. She had been increasing her targeted number of laps to ten lately, but this time she wasn't even counting. Her mind was on the talk with Paige and her body was experiencing one of those zones of energy that long distance athletes savor: sweet effortless motion. As soon as she showered and dressed she texted Paige: "We gotta get together. How about four o'clock at home?" She had swum twenty-four laps.

Joyce thanked her daughter again and again for coming to her. And "for being such a good person." She added, "When I was swimming this morning the picture of your little group–what do you call yourselves? . . ."

". . . Troublemakers. . ."

". . . came to me. They could be a help, but I think you need to invite a couple more to join you. Like Chris and Sharon."

"And you!" Paige exclaimed.

"That's sweet of you, darling. I'd rather stay on the side lines, but may I suggest an agenda item for you to consider?"

"Sure."

"Start out with that exercise you did in class. What do you call it?"

"'Don't Hold Back!'"

"Yeah. And about Sharon living with us? My precious daughter, I don't know about that one."

Trouble Makers Meet

They were all there very early, the Trouble Makers. On Lombardi Time. Green Bay Packers legendary coach Vince Lombardi was so passionate (compulsive? anal?) about starting a meeting punctually, that if he called one for, say 8:00 a.m.–the time of this one–anyone who appeared after 7:55 was considered late. Veteran Trouble Makers Paige, Jayne, Alan, Carleton, and Keyshawn as well as newcomers Sharon and Chris were all seated and ready to roll by ten to eight. Chris was inwardly delighted to join this shadow clique and offered to hold the meeting in his office. Paige, in her role as leader, accepted and messages were sent out. She said it was to be a one item meeting, and described their task as "doing some big-time planning on behalf of Belle Waters's homeless."

Paige welcomed newcomers Sharon and Chris. She introduced Sharon as a fine friend full of ideas from High School. Together Paige and Sharon described the Don't Hold Back! exercise used at school, and then Paige presented wording for a problem to be addressed.

She said, "Let's come away from this morning with specific ideas on how our church can ratchet up combatting homelessness. Hosting families for a week helps every once in a while like in Helping Hands, and I don't want to take away from the wonderful efforts of a lot of people–including my mother–who work their–well, who work hard, but I think we all agree that something more could be done, right?"

Everyone nodded.

"So, I'm going to throw out this problem for us to solve." Slowly she enunciated "How can we make a difference in the efforts to help the homeless people of our town? Considering our mental, physical, and financial resources, how can Fair Are the Meadows church support something that has long-term gains for homeless people, and considering what we know about the homeless, what can we ask them to bring to the effort? How can they contribute?

"Let's begin by firing out various specific ideas. Short bits at first. Then we can tie them together, and remember these ground rules: no premature criticism, hook your ideas on to others, and the wilder the better. Let's not think of any of them as impossible, at least in this first round. And let's get a lot of them. Ready? Set! Go!" The Trouble Makers fired away:

"Invite homeless guests to stay in our homes."
"Provide apartments at church."
"Build new homes, like in Habitat for Humanity."
"Recruit mentors."
"Teach them golf. The homeless ones."
"Require them to teach us some things."
"Collaborate with other churches or non-profits (or profits!) to do something big."
"Create a job placement service. We could tally things the homeless kids would do for pay."
"Lobby the state of Wisconsin to pass a law to allow sixteen-year-olds to legally consent for admission to a shelter or transitional program. Now

they have to wait until they're eighteen, and yet most homeless kids, like those in the 16:49 program at the high school are younger than that."

"Have golfing mentors. Use the golfing culture of Meadows to attract homeless kids and make the helping part fun for our members."

"Caddying. Caddying. Caddying."

"Yeah, we could invite them in, teach them some golf, and give free lessons to their families or friends."

"How about having homeless kids work for their room and board, and then have them acquire a stake in it. Like a cooperative. Shares. Stocks."

"How about keeping up the Helping Hands program as is, but add to it a home-based program where members commit to having a homeless person in their house for a period of time, like a month or week or something."

"Let's think of having a board of directors where some homeless kids have to be voting members . . ."

". . . and alums of the program could stay on to share their experience and wisdom."

"Could we collaborate with Belle Waters College? How about a tutoring program with some of their departments, or sororities, or fraternities?"

"How about a Belle Waters College sports team taking on a certain number of kids as mentees, who do some sort of service in return?"

"Did we mention a listing of homeless skills matched to the talents of the church members?"

"Let's ask a lot–a real lot–of our members. Make membership physical, like the Marines."

"How about an on-line Kick Starter campaign to get us off the ground financially?"

"We can certainly have social media accounts to generate support beyond the church."

"We're talking about ownership here, aren't we? Let's help them have a stake in what we do."

"Let's collaborate with the golf courses around here and offer junior memberships for our homeless kids in exchange for some work they could do. This may involve caddying, but there are a lot of other things that need to be done at a golf course. It's a business."

"How about a talent show that pairs a homeless child with a member? A member-mentor fund-raiser."

"How about a–I might call it an–entrepreneur category for our kids? Help them pull out new ideas for helping our effort."

"What might we name this project? Vagrants Victorious? Possessing the Dispossessed? Destitute Institute? Misplaced Love? Up and In (Like down & out)? Potent-shall-we? Budding Buddies? High Capacity City? Up with this town? Showing off our potent-shells?"

* * *

These Trouble Makers were disciplined. They never criticized what others said but of course some of the ideas were throw-aways. Forty-five minutes whizzed by, and Paige saw some of them looking at their watches. "Okay," she said, "Let me and Sharon pull some ideas together, share them with you on line, and then we'll get together to take our next steps."

Everyone was fine with that, but Sharon quietly interrupted and said, "Not all of us have easy access to the internet." Alan and Carleton smiled.

Paige said, "Whoops. I'll get together with you one way or another. I promise."

As the adults left they praised what they called the girls' incredible leadership and energy. Outside, Carleton leaned over toward Alan and whispered, "We've got to tell the others about our backgrounds. How we became homeless."

Alan stared at him and finally said, "I don't know about that one."

9

Crunch Time

Dreaming

CHRIS JUST HAD TO talk with his golfing guru after the roller coaster experiences of the last two times out on the course. Gentry was waiting in his office at the Community Center leaning back in his swivel desk chair, finger tips together, with pursed lips. It was a caricature of a psychiatrist ready to soak up his client. He listened–after their handshakes and how are you's–as Chris rat-a-tatted a summary–of recent highs and lows.

"You should have seen me when I had the seventy-four!" Chris started out, and waited for a response that didn't come. He went on. "Ok, I got lucky with the three hole-outs from off the green, but even if I sank nothing and had one putts on those holes, I would have had a seventy-seven. *Two* putts on each of those holes would have given me an eighty. I was only aiming to break ninety that day. But a seventy-four! A seventy-seven? An eighty? All of them would have been miracles."

"Manna from heaven," Gentry said softly.

Chris continued a bit more relaxed. "I don't think it was pure luck that put me what, four standard deviations beyond what I would be expected to score considering my–what should we call it–skill level?"

"Handicap," Gentry said.

Chris said, "My body was moving freely and on that back nine, the only swing thought I had over the ball was: Tempo with vision. Picture the swing. Keep that wonderful rhythm. Relax and savor what I have here, wherever it is coming from. Don't fiddle around. Hit the ball, now. And it stayed with me that whole back nine for a two under par thirty-two."

He paused waiting for a response, but the teacher just looked at him and finally said, "That's a lot of swing thoughts. You couldn't have had all

that going on at once and play the way you did. It was something else. Some
unifying force or other."

Chris wasn't listening. "But then there was the 101," he said head down
in mock supplication. "I suppose you've heard about that one." He looked
up. Gentry was nodding.

"Well, I couldn't do anything that day. If I had to blame my problem on
any one factor it would be that Jayne was with me and I wanted to impress
her. I have to admit that I bragged so much about the seventy-four that there
was pressure on me to keep playing well. But it has to be more than that,
doesn't it, Professor? . . . Doctor? . . . Counselor?"

Gentry looked at him stone faced and Chris continued.

"I was tight and anxious. I froze on chips and putts, but even the full
shots had the vice grip of what do they call it? The yips?"

Gentry nodded.

"I was humiliated out there in front of somebody who I wanted to
impress–whom –, and she was making fun of me, but I guess I provided her
with raw material."

Gentry smiled.

"Chris finished his confessional with, "So what do you think? How do
I get back on track?"

Gentry leaned back with his hands clasped behind his head, looked at
the ceiling for a long moment, and said, "Let me tell you about the dream I
had a few nights ago. You can be my psychoanalyst and interpret it, or not.
Then we'll get back to *your* golf."

Slowly the words came out of this teacher's mouth.

"I was caddying for Iron Byron, you know, that mechanical robot swing
machine who always hits the ball straight, like Byron Nelson did. I would
have named the machine after Mo Norman. Iron Mo they could call him,
but my subconscious mind chose Mr. Nelson. Well, I have to say that this
Iron Byron wonderfully does what all fine golfers do as their downswings get
into the hitting area: apply power coming out of a lag that releases squarely
to the club face. It works for all good golfers and for this robot.

"The real mechanical Iron Byron is fastened onto a firm pedestal, but
in my dream, he moved along kinda like a Segue scooter, and I was his
caddy at Sandy Hollow golf course down in Rockford tagging along side but
sometimes unable to keep up with him as he hit perfect shot after perfect
shot, and then rushed off to hit the next one. I scooted after it–him. He
looked impatiently back at me. I was puffing trying to keep up. He was playing fine golf. On the first nine he went 434 343 325 for a four-under par 31.
He walked the walk you might say, that Byron.

"Well, as we went from the ninth green to the tenth tee, he saw some-body he knew and waved. It was a robotic character like R2D2, and he lost track of where he was going and tripped, falling flat on his face. Iron Byron did. R2D2 came over and fiddled with his body. He may have been repairing it. I didn't dare interfere with what they were doing, I being a mere caddy. You understand?"

Chris nodded.

"Well, Byron's drive on number ten went out of bounds. So did his next one, and the next. He switched from a driver to a five iron for his sev-enth shot and with a funny uncoordinated swing he kind of bunted the ball down the left side of the fairway away from the big trap on the right. He managed to get twelve on this short par four with a lucky third putt, and walked to the eleventh tee with a pout on his face. I was lagging behind very confused. Now number eleven at Sandy Hollow is a short par three with a pond in front. Byron asked me for a different ball, and proceeded to skull his eight iron into the water. From the drop area, he took a 60-degree wedge for his third and plopped it in again. He looked at me as if I was the cause of his dramatic descent into, well, wouldn't this be way down in the nether regions, Pastor Ek?"

"Sure."

"So, I said to him. This is your last ball, Iron Byron. I mean sir. He was incensed, grabbed it from me, and promptly chunked that one into the water too. When he held his hand out to me for another ball, I said that I told you that one was the last one we had, and he fired me. He just said: 'Go!' And I woke up. Sweating, but then laughing hard and long. So, what do you think of that, Pastor Ek? What does it mean?"

Relaxed now, Chris grinned and said, "I think I know–you're anxious about something–but you have to hear *my* dream now. Okay? Then we can talk about both of them. This happened just last night," Chris said, eager to start.

"I was all ready to give what I thought was a terrific sermon. I had been planning and practicing it all week, even sharing a run-through with Jayne. The theme was based on peeling an onion. You know, like when you go to the next layer and the next and the next, you finally get to the last one and there's nothing left. The layers *are* the onion. And you are crying. Well, I thought it had nice theological parallels about going somewhere without an end in sight or finding out that what you have been investing your time or energy in has no future or something like that. In the dream, the sermon and the service into which it was placed was so important to me that I didn't even want to farm out the liturgy to somebody else, so contrary to my recent practice I did the readings myself. One was from Deuteronomy 8 about the wealth of our lives as a gift, and another from First Chronicles 29 about the giving required to build the temple, the house of God. Keep in mind that this was not a Stewardship Sunday. I was aiming at something beyond that, like the real meaning of what we are here on Earth to do. Understand?"

Gentry nodded.

"They were moving along famously, the service and the sermon. I had everyone's attention from the beginning. People chuckled and kept quiet at all the right moments, and they seem to understand what I was trying to get across. It was, I must say, the best service and the finest response that I had ever had at Meadows. But then as I made a grand hand gesture, I brushed against my microphone and it got all discombobulated. Everything fell apart: The equipment, my concentration, the behavior of the congregation, and my sermon.

"This is so goofy: Words then started coming out of my mouth a split second after I said them, and sometimes my voice would sound like I had inhaled nitrogen or laughing gas. I talked like Donald Duck. The congregation looked side to side at each other, as if they were trying to figure out what was happening, and I seemed to be out of the picture. None of them paid any attention to me anymore. I kept up my delayed, quacking voice and they kept searching for the answer to what was happening without paying any attention to me. Then, Ebby Stone called out in an enormous voice *Time for the offering*! And I slumped out a door at the front of the sanctuary, leaned against a wall, and cried.

"I woke up with a physical start. First feeling relieved and then terrified. I'm not kidding. What do you think it meant?"

Keyshawn Gentry was quick to respond this time. "They're the same. Your dream and mine. They're wake-up calls, like many dreams. They shove fears right at us that we may not have been paying enough attention to in our waking hours. As a golf professional, I am concerned when my students struggle with the game. When they are completely lost–like when they shoot 75 and then 105 in consecutive rounds."

"I shot 74 and 101."

"I know. I know. That was just an example. Don't be so wrapped up in yourself," Gentry said with an attitude he could not suppress.

"When my golfing students are lost, I feel lost. I have an obligation to help them, but at the same time I realize that they are just trying to do their best at something that–let's face it–is only a game. It really is, of course. Golf gets greatly exaggerated as a metaphor for life, but let me say this: I do not like it when people hate golf because it's allegedly a rich person's game. Golf has inherent value and appeal no matter how rich you are. It is one of the many worthwhile joys of life. Do the same critics who rail at golf rail at art or dance or theater because rich folks patronize them? I don't think so."

Gentry was getting off topic, but Chris listened patiently. He really did respect and love this guy, and thought, *"He has every right to drift off topic, just like all preachers at one time or another."*

They had shared their personal stories and were heard. The session was a success.

Feedback from the governing board

Unbeknownst to Christopher Ek at this time, the governing board, led by Eberhard Stone, was getting itchy to develop an evaluation of his performance. So, when their pastor was attending meetings of the Wisconsin United Church of Christ conference in the Dells, the board got together and manufactured a questionnaire. Each of them filled it out on-line in the privacy of their homes and sent it to their leader.

Results of the instrument would be shared with Chris and used to provide raw material for a conversation with him. It was slapped together and unscientific, but they and Pastor Ek were on record as wanting candid feedback from each other. When they hired him, they said that they would be evaluating him periodically, so this exercise in feedback should not be a surprise. More pertinent to its timing was the fact that complaints aimed at Chris were emerging. His honeymoon was over.

Some members were concerned about his golf, others about his "losing control of the youth," and one about his relationship with Jayne Nova. She was allegedly spending the night with him at his apartment. In a testy retort to this rumor, one of Chris's most loyal supporters said. "She wasn't actually seen there, but her droolingly seductive Miata was observed parked in front of his place early in the morning when–I'll call her Mrs. X–conveniently took a detour from her usual early morning walk and saw it up close. I hear she took a license number that day and had her cop-husband check it out. It was Ms. Nova's. So what. We aren't the morality police, or are we? In this day and age can't a young single all-American clergyman be alive? Fully alive?"

A student member of the board added, "Or a clergy member of any demographic or gender group!"

The instrument along with the board's responses looked like this:

Pastor Assessment Questionnaire

of Christopher Hilding Ek

of Fair Are the Meadows UCC Church

Please rate Christopher Ek on a scale of 1 to 5, where 5 is the best, in each of these categories. Comment as appropriate. All responses will remain anonymous.

To what extent is Pastor Ek reaching out to all members of the congregation? (Median rating: 2)

Comments

"Those who come to church regularly have every opportunity to interact with Pastor C. He is always available in the back of the church after services or in the Riley Room afterwards."

"I've heard–I don't know this for sure–that he doesn't recruit for new members much, and that some homebound people and those in assisted living places complain that he's never out to visit them."

"He is so young. What is he, twenty-six or seven? I have a grand-child his age. He is a pleasant guy, but what can I learn from him?"

"I've heard that if you want some time with Pastor Chris, go to the Muni Golf course clubhouse after ten on a Monday."

"I see him anytime I want to. I don't know what people are complaining about. Actually, maybe they're not. I haven't heard anything, anyway."

"I don't think that 'reaching out' necessarily is a primary job of the pastor. We members should do that. I often think we don't do it enough, but I must say that I'm guilty of this omission as much as anyone."

"The profile of this church has improved so much during Chris's time with us. We are becoming a country club church. Yippee! (I've always wanted to be thought of as rich!) I see more people in the pews on Sunday morning, and I swear that some of them still have their golf shoes on. Our rugs are getting rattier."

"He is a prince of a young man. We are so fortunate to have him."

"You know, I just don't know. I liked him so much at first, but doubts are creeping in."

To what extent is Pastor Ek knowledgeable regarding the Bible?
(Median rating: 3)

Comments

"I like the way his scripture readings match his sermons, but maybe that's because the common scripture–what do they call it, the lectionary?–guides him. Does he have a lot of freedom in choosing those passages? I wish somebody other than his girl-friend would do the readings for the day."

"I love the way that Jayne–I can't remember her last name–does the liturgy. She's a dynamo. I'm no youngster by any means (I won't say just how many years have gone by since my baptism) and my hearing leaves something to be desired, but I can hear Jayne when she reads. What good is any message if you can't hear it? Are my comments here on the topic of Pastor C's knowl-edge of the Bible? Maybe not, but it's the first thing that comes to me in reading the question, so I have to put it down."

"I honestly don't think Chris Ek knows much about the Bible. I'll bet our Ebby Stone knows more, or at least can quote more. He–Chris–hardly ever uses the Bible after the scripture read-ings, but I have to say that his words in the sermon are so beauti-fully related to the music selections and the scriptures. I get a lot out of his sermons."

"Sometimes I wonder if our pastor ever even reads the Bible. Most of the time you might as well be a Unitarian around here."

"I love Pastor Ek. Because of him, I am reading the Gospel of John. Wow. That thing is wild. I'm a late-in-life church goer and never had confronted it–John–before."

"From the start, I assumed that Chris was very knowledgeable about the Bible and Biblical scholarship, in large part because I know that he came through the Chicago Theological Seminary, and they must have high standards (Mustn't they?). He hasn't let me down. His comments from the pulpit reveal a sensitivity to sources as well as a good spirit regarding the Bible. So, I'd say he does know the Bible, and while that may not necessarily be important to a lot of us UCCers, it is to me."

"I don't know or care if Chris is knowledgeable about the Bible. I think he cares about us on Sunday morning, and his sermons certainly express the essence of the Bible as I want it to be, anyway. We cherry pick from that it anyway. I'll bet somewhere out in academia there's a book written that shows so many both hurtful (hateful?) and loving passages, that it must seem like two different books. These days I'm not afraid of admitting that the Bible doesn't mean much to me. When we were in confirmation class we were taught to almost worship it. '*Never put another book on top of the Bible. Capitalize its title.*' Comments like that. But I babble. Chris's knowledge about the Bible is just fine with me."

"I wish we used the Cotton Patch Bible in this church."

"I wish somebody would write a short 'Bible' about learning about life from golf. Based on Harvey Penick or Mo Norman. Hey, maybe they have: *Golf in the Kingdom*?"

To what extent is he sensitive to matters
other than those that involve Sunday morning?
(like the physical condition of our building and grounds, the performance of
the rest of the staff: our clerical assistant, our janitor, our choir director, etc.)
(Median rating: 3)

Comments

"Why should he be? *We* should handle that: the laity. One of us should be responsible for keeping tabs on the personnel, another one for the . . . I guess it's called buildings and grounds. I think it's ridiculous that we even have a question like this as part of Chris's evaluation. Let's get with it, folks!"

"This building is always clean–I think it is, anyway, but my standards may be low, and the staff is wonderful. So is Chris. Is he on 'the staff,' actually, or is he in another more lofted category?"

"Chris needs to spend a lot more time on these matters. What does he do during the week, anyway?"

"If Sandy hadn't left us, I think she should've been promoted and given a new assignment to keep on top of the building's condition, but not the music."

"The music is soooo good in this church. Let's just keep it the way it is and keep Chris from sticking his nose into it."

"Chris works so well with the organist and choir. And he seems to already know some of the part time musicians we hire. Kudos to Chris."

"We need to update our committees and get them–us–to do more around here. I don't think we ask enough of our people when they become members. Sorry to say it, but that includes us on the board."

"I'll admit that we and most churches ask a lot of clergy, too much. But that's the way it is these days and people who go into preaching should be aware of it and be prepared. I'll bet that the young ministers who are on top of the cleanliness of their church (Chris isn't) and the coordination of preaching and music (He is) get good marks from people like us."

"He's not sensitive to these issues. I think he's in a world of his own, and–I know this will sound funny–too much involved with making his Sunday sermons work."

Does he golf too much?
(Median rating: 3)

Comments

"Yes, without a doubt. It's gotten to a point where when people talk about our church that four-letter word G-O-L-F always comes up. I don't like it."

"My understanding of this question is unclear. Does a rating of 5 mean that I like golfing a lot or what? Or, what about a 1? I for one wish he would golf to his heart's content. More if that's what turns him on. The fact–I repeat *fact*–is that since Chris's arrival we are regarded as a golfing congregation–not necessarily a Country Club Church, but I suppose that's possible. Since he came I suspect we have more members and we definitely have more people sitting in the pews. I've seen some that look like early Sunday morning public course guys who haven't had time to take a shower yet, and I know that people talk more about us around town. That's good. There. I've had my say. I've wanted to get this off my chest for a long time."

"Of course, he golfs too much. It's an embarrassment to Meadows. It's the main thing non-members from the town talk about when they see me and know that I go here. I think we should confront him about it. I might as well come clean and say that I don't like golf. It's a game of the rich, by the rich, and for the rich."

"I have bitten my tongue while listening to some of our members rail on and on about Chris's fascination with golf. They call it a rich person's pursuit that has no place in a UCC church, but–listen to this–would they, *do they,* use the same standard if a minister is gung ho about the arts which is also a pet pursuit of wealthy folks? I don't think so. Good grief, let's let the guy do his own thing. Rich people have lots of choices in their lives. Golf wouldn't have become so associated with them if it were all bad."

"I love the way that he and the youth of the church have sponsored some golf outings. Look, I sometimes gag at the way that anything mentioning the Packers gets laughs and applause. Let's give golf a break. If anything, it is declining as an activity, partly because Tiger Woods is no longer the only alpha male out there. That worries me. Golf is worth keeping. So are public courses that beautify neighborhoods. So there!"

"What a stupid question. Who cares what he does on his free time."

"No."

"Nope."

"I liked it when he first came here and shared some golfing stories from the pulpit, but I think he may have done one too many for me.

His way of doing liturgy.
(Median rating: 4)

Comments

"I love the way he does the liturgy, the scripture reading any-way–farming it out–and the way he puts Biblical passages on the marquee during the week gets me thinking about the service ahead of Sundays."

"Let's assign a liturgist each week or month or year or whatever and have them do it respectfully. Not a show-off like that Jayne who struts around with her . . . well, I could say more but I want to be respectful to those of you reading this. It really gets under my skin, the pushy way she goes up there in front and speaks in her overly enunciated tones."

"I listen to the liturgy. I didn't use to. And it is so much a part of his sermons. Kudos to Chris. And Jayne Nova. She does a great job."

"I like it, but I wish we could go beyond the Bible for selections. There is so much wisdom in, oh, fiction, and the classics. Don't get me wrong. I'm not a–what do they call it these days–'None of the above,' but I have to say that sometimes our Christianity is limiting. There is so much out there in addition to us. Maybe we should think of ourselves as first among equals, but let some of the equals be heard. I babble on, but for a long time, I've been wanting to say this somehow."

"I think that Pastor Ek nicely coordinates the liturgy and service. He puts thought into how they can work together, and it works for me."

"I'm a former Lutheran as you all know so I'm used to sung liturgy. I wish we could do it at Meadows. But let's choose good melodies that stick with us during the week. I suspect that Pastor Chris would be daring enough to sing some of them on his own, like a cantor. He has a pretty good voice."

"In my opinion Chris is a good preacher, but I have always thought that preaching gets too much attention or emphasis is our services. Don't the Episcopalians have a very liturgical service? We have the freedom to have more singing. Don't Mennonites do that? I think we once had some people in this church who grew up singing many parts in the hymns. They called themselves Mennonites, I think. Something like that."

"He's doing just fine in every way."

"How much freedom does Meadows or Chris have in choosing scripture readings? I wish we would let the youth of the church make suggestions. We may regret it sometimes, but I suspect that they would feel more a part of the congregation. Like maybe they would pick words from their favorite songs."

His relationship with the youth of our church.
(Median rating: 4.5)

Comments

"That Paige is a piece of work. I don't know if I would want her in any class I teach. She is so opinionated and cheeky. She acts like she knows more about religion and life, than anyone around here including Chris. Well, maybe she does, but I don't think Chris has control of her."

"Okay, enough of this confidentiality. I am a youth member of this board and a member of Pastor Ek's class. My opinion of him has changed and maybe is still changing. At first, I thought that he was weird and unorganized. Now I almost worship him, but my parents tell me to be careful about that. I have to say, however, that Pastor Ek–I feel I should use a formal manner of address in this official comment–Pastor Ek has drawn us out. We all are free to say what we are thinking about religion or whatever, and we listen to each other. This is a very important point because everywhere outside of this church, we are in a culture that yells and interrupts. I give Pastor Ek credit for developing this listening quality in us. Maybe it's mindfulness? From the start, he would take us seriously no matter what we said. When he listened to a silly or obviously inappropriate comment and gave the speaker a chance to get it out without the rest of us dissing them, he was genuine. He practiced what he preached. Listen. Think. Don't hold back (But he says he is working on this one himself and finds us–kids–better than him.) I could go on and on. I do adore *Christ*opher Ek. In some touching moments, I think he's like Jesus must have been. That's silly, perhaps, but I have to say it. I mean it today. Will I mean it when I am Pastor Ek's age or my parents' age? Don't know."

"There seems to be more interest on the part of the youth of the church these days. I don't know if there are more of them–kids–here, but they seem downright enthused about church. Amazing."

"They're doing fine. I like what I hear about them–the kids–but I'm so old that youth groups are three or four generations removed from what concerns me these days. How about if we start an 'old' group? An organized bunch of us that regularly tries to confront the issues of being 90 or 80 or 70 or 60? I know, age is not just chronological, but do you get what I'm trying to say? I guess it's this: I'm more worried about our unintentional 'age-ism' than youth groups. They are sailing along. We old farts are taking on water. How about a sermon about Noah bringing aboard two octogenarians when the flood came?"

"Our kids are involved in church more than at any time in my memory, including when I was a kid, and I don't think I'm compromising anonymity to say that I won't see sixty again. I think that they may be seriously looking at the matter of homelessness. I know one of them who is as into that stuff as others are with social media or soccer. Chris deserves credit for this. He provides opportunities for them and I think enough of them have taken

advantage of it that we can say that the youth program at Meadows is working. And let's give credit where credit is due. To Chris,
but golf is a force too. I am not a fan of that–what do they call
it–game, but the self-discipline and good exercise they get from
it is pretty amazing in my eyes. And those people the kids work
with–Keyshawn Gentry and the other black guys–are amazing,
and they come to church. It sounds crazy but homeless people
have become role models for our children. I think our golfing pastor deserves an A+ in his work with young people, but we must
recognize that he's not doing it alone. They learn from God but
also from golf, . . . the kids."

"I wish I could say I agree with our pastor's approach to youth. It's
got people interested and kind of energized, I guess. But here's my
take: Is our youth program any different from a secular approach
to doing good? At its heart, isn't it kinda like something that could
come out of a public school or a boys and girls club or maybe the
boy scouts or girl scouts. Is there still a girl scouts or program
around here in Belle Waters? Why don't we have them in this
church? Boy scouts and girl scouts? When I went to church as a
kid we boy scouts could earn something called Pro Deo et Patria.
I think that means for God and the father land or something like
that. It was religious but also patriotic. Our church–Meadows–is
not patriotic. Not overtly so, but not–is there a word–*covertly* so
either. We don't even have the American flag displayed. Are we
trying to avoid it? I sometimes think we try to avoid any reference
to anything that could be interpreted as Republican, while the
Democratic words are all over the place. Diversity. Giving. Sexism. Patriarchy. Why don't we just come out and say it–like that
Unitarian church in Rockford does over public radio–that we are
a bunch of liberals? Are we afraid to say that we love our country?
Look, I was never for Trump or Scott Walker or Paul Ryan–well,
I did like Paul Ryan at times and I'm interested in his place in
history. I remember when he spoke to Belle Waters Rotary years
and years ago when was going for his first term in Congress. He
looked like he was eighteen years old, but he was really twenty-
eight. I think he's a Catholic. They must have had a good youth
program at church. He could certainly have earned a Pro Deo et
Patria award. Am I making sense? Look, I really like Fair Are the
Meadows Family Church–I wouldn't be going here and pledging
money if I didn't–but I think Pastor Ek and our youth program (I
almost wrote pogrom. Freudian slip?) could be offered outside of
a church. Am I making sense?"

Does he meet your expectations as a minister
considering our congregational goals in hiring him?
(Average response: 4.0).

Comments:

"Yes, absolutely."

"We have asked him to do many things and he has worked hard and accomplished a lot."

"He's just a beginner. Let's not be too harsh on him."

"I think it's too early to be doing an evaluation like this."

"I'm not going to comment on this one."

"Of course (bad pun regarding the golfer that occupies our pulpit!). We are lucky to have him, golfing or not."

"Let's lengthen his contract and give him a big raise. When people talk about him or his golf, it's always with a smile. They like him whether we do or not. Let's be gentle. He's only a kid."

"Most of the time, yes."

"I think we made a mistake hiring this young man. I can't remember who was on the search committee, but I sure wasn't. And he's way too direct with us–too candid about some of that searching stuff. If he hasn't found it yet, how are we supposed to? I want a pastor who is my spiritual guide. Somebody who is way ahead of me in things religious. This guy's not."

Chris was crushed when in the privacy of his office he read the results. He got hot all over and felt that his blood pressure was really high. Maybe it was because the last quote under the expectations question was so negative, like it was a summary. He admitted to himself upon re-reading everything several times that the rankings and most of the comments were really quite good and reasonable. Later in the day his emotions gave way to the sober realization that people perceive him and religion and age groups in so many ways. How can anyone–even an experienced minister–deal with that? He thought of Keyshawn Gentry's line: *Be yourself, but let yourself grow.* Good advice for golf and life.

10

Peeling Onions

Peeling Onions: The Sermon

RIGHT AFTER THE ANNOUNCEMENTS and without any introductory scripture readings, Pastor Ek launched into a sermon that he called Peeling Onions. He talked about how when a vexing issue finally goes away, there will always be another waiting to take its place. Like the next layer of an onion. Looking us in the eyes and sometimes making us cry. He gave examples: After we get a good mark on a dreaded test, the positive vibes soon become nudged aside by the emerging pain that comes from being shunned by somebody who used to be our friend. Or after an overdrawn bank account is reconciled and the accompanying anxiety goes away, we realize that we forgot to call our aging parents when they expected it last night. Or an hour or so after the relief of getting a good report from a medical test wears off, we feel a puzzling pain in some new part of our bodies. It always happens. Successive dilemmas are waiting to grab our attention, and sometimes they make us cry.

Then enunciating in slow motion, he said that when these all appear to be under control, you can address the biggest one of all: "Your golf game. It's enough to make you weep uncontrollably." Chris waited, expecting a jovial response, but everyone stayed quiet and stared back at him.

It caught him off guard. He had wanted to bring down the house with his punch line and get a roar of laughter in return. He never dreamed that this gesture at humor would be received with anything but joy. Pawing at notes, he said, "If you peel an onion again and again, it will disappear. There is nothing at its core. The same can happen to us: Bad news piled on bad news or frustration upon frustration can leave us with empty despair. And nothing to hold on to. Without a core. Or a safety net. Or a lighthouse. Or a savior."

He continued to stammer with his head down squinting at scribbles on little cards. "We best function if these challenges are addressed with truth and candor, but then there are always those others waiting for us. At least for adults. Babies and young kids and perhaps even teenagers are immune, I suspect. How about it?" he asked, scanning the pews for one of his young charges.

Paige called out, "I'm thinking. I'm thinking." Everyone laughed the way Chris wanted them to respond to the golf comment.

So was he. Thinking. Paige's interruption gave him a few seconds to re-boot. Looking out at the congregation he asked, "When you solve it, are you complete? Are you whole? Are you content?" How about it, young people? What do you think? Give us some examples."

They responded. Back and forth the youth of the church called out things that bother them, but then disappear for a while. Big matters and small–layers of the onion–that are peeled away only to reveal new difficulties waiting in the wings to be contemplated:

"Bullying."

"Screwing up for the team."

"Being misunderstood."

"Not getting into a group."

"Acne."

"Saying something stupid."

"Denting a parent's car."

Chris laughed at this last one, because he had done that, but nobody else did. At least out loud. Then he said, "For big people, big issues. For little people, little ones," and immediately wanted to take back his words.

"That is not necessarily true," Paige called out. "We so-called little people can have some big challenges–at least they seem that way to us–but I send out a loud amen to most of what you have said."

Many in the congregation joined in. "Amen."

Chris smiled, gave Paige a thumbs up, and tried to compare onions to something bigger. "When you get to the end of peeling the onion, there's nothing there," he said. "But for us Christians, there is always something even in the darkest times when there is no solution staring us in the faith, I mean face." Now everyone laughed, hard and long.

Straight faced, he continued. "It's from the Bible, the New Testament and the Old. Let's listen to the wisdom that comes from that Holy Book this morning." He pointed toward a cluster of his young charges who had been in on the planning of this part of the service.

George began. "For God so loved the world that he gave his one and only Son, that whoever believes in him shall not perish but have eternal life. John 3:16"

Gloria said that if you confess with your mouth that Jesus is Lord, and believe in your heart that God raised him from the dead, you will be saved. She went on, "I am the way, the truth and the life. No one comes to the Father except through me. John 14:6"

Then slowly together all of them chanted,

"So, do not fear, for I am with you; do not be dismayed, for I am your God. I will strengthen you and help you. Isa 41:10."

"Let the peace of Christ rule in your hearts. Col 3:15."

"Trust in the Lord and lean not on your own understanding. Prov 3:5."

The congregation applauded. Jayne thought it was cheesy and stupid–this need to give immediate affirmation through clapping–and put her hands into her pockets.

The line to shake Pastor Ek's hand after the service was long. A lot of them said they liked the sermon and the kids' participation. Jayne waited patiently with the others. As she shook Chris's hands she leaned in and whispered, "Have you ever heard of Maslow's Hierarchy of Needs? It would give you new energy and space the next time you do this sermon."

And she did this. Then and there while holding his hand firmly and talking fast, she pushed back at Pastor Chris's onion metaphor by summarizing a model of *ascending* steps toward the good life. She said that if physiological necessities that keep us alive and safe are met, then we can move upward fulfilling subsequent needs for group affiliation, then esteem and maybe, if we're fortunate, we can experience self-actualization. Being all that we can be. Maximizing our potential. She was trying to describe extreme human behavior. Some people can barely get a toehold on the first rung of the ladder while others reach beyond the highest one: "Us!" she emphasized as her voice dropped to a whisper. "From the extreme of the homeless not having their basic needs met to us middle class educated types who want to become all wise." She squeezed his hand even harder and closed with, "How about a walk today, after lunch?"

Jayne picked up where she left off as they ambled along the river on that sleepy Sunday afternoon. "Please don't think of me as patronizing, Chris. I suspect you know about these things, but I have to have my say in light of what you fired at us from the pulpit. The point is this: we are so privileged, you and I and almost all of those who sit in your pews. Our unmet needs don't relate to food or shelter or protecting our bodies from attack. Okay, we can be ill and we can walk in dangerous places, but we have the resources to take care of ourselves when we do. When I choose to go to church to hear a stimulating message, like I expect from you, I'm pining for intellectual challenge. I want to grow. I want to learn those things that so much of the world must consider frills. The arts. Ethical systems. History. Magnanimity. How we are put together. And of course, golf."

She stopped suddenly, smiled, and said, "I know I must be preaching to a choir of one here. You. But thanks for listening."

"No, no, that is more than okay," he said. "Hey. I need feedback about my sermons, and what you are saying sure fits in. You know, this layer stuff reminds me of a conversation I had with my grandfather over lunch once after we played golf. I call him G'Pa. We were alone at a corner table of the clubhouse gulping our first beers when he started crying. Tears were rolling down his face. I reached for his hand and held it. I said, 'What's the matter?'

He took a while to get it out, and said, 'I'm so happy, Chris. I love you so much and being with you–like right now–is heaven on earth for me.'

"I didn't know how to respond. Finally, I said, 'Could you tell me more, G'Pa?'

"He blew his nose, gave me his big smile, and said, 'Chris, I am so bliss-ful these days. Everything is going so unbelievably well, and yet I'm so old. Do you know how old I am? Well, it's a pretty respectable score for eighteen holes.' He looked at me, and I smiled. He continued. 'These days people like me think about our health a lot. If it isn't the heart, it's the memory or the sciatic nerve or the teeth or the skin or the constipation–or the runs–signs of old mortal coils unraveling. And if it isn't the fragile health it's the high cost of things–too little money chasing too many bills and too many dreams of exotic travel–or what we are going to do with all the things we have? And it's the friends my age who are dying from natural causes. Of course, I always read the obits in our little paper down at The Villages, and I can't help but notice how young those people are. The dead ones.' He reached over and started rubbing my shoulder like he did when I was very young.

"'Well,' he said, 'here's the thing. When you called me a couple of days ago to suggest playing golf today I was pre-occupied with several of these ominous concerns. I didn't appreciate the priceless gift of being with my grandson. Today–now–I do and these tears are telling me how precious you are.'"

Jayne had been listening intently. Then she said, "But what does this have to do with onions, or Maslow, or the things you and I were just talk-ing about?"

"I'm getting to that. My grandfather said that when he is pre-occupied with his health or finances or what he calls stupid little matters, he isn't ap-propriately appreciating the things that really count, like his family. Like me and the wonderful relationship we have. But when he is freed of these things by putting them in their place or by truly feeling healthy and as secure as one can be once in a while at his stage in life, the value of our family jumps to the head of the parade of–he calls it–life flying by. He is free to put things in their proper order. G'Pa said, 'I can't just turn a switch and fully appreciate my family or the really important other things that have been a part of my life. I have to first feel good and have those other things under control. Or at least think they are. Do you understand?' he said to me.

"And I did," Chris said to Jayne. "It's like the onion business and your Maslow. The foundation has to be there."

Jayne said, "I'd like to meet your grandparents someday." Her eyes were misty.

Years later when Chris would think back to Jayne and that walk, he inevitably would hear the words, "No stars above, but still I fell in love on a sleepy Sunday afternoon," to the tune usually associated with *Country Gardens*. But then he would think, "but was I really in love?"

The onion sermon was personal and important to Chris, but he knew he had screwed it up. He stumbled and mumbled, and the kids saved him. And then there was Jayne's exegesis and his reflections on the relationship with G'Pa. He concluded that sermons are never complete. The big ones, anyway. There's always a new chapter or verse waiting to build on. Thank goodness for that.

He was learning something, but his layers of longing and loss had been piling on top of each other: his relationship with Jayne (unresolved), his progress in leading Meadows down a path to successfully address the matter of homelessness (unresolved), and his own faith: He wasn't sure that he was as faithful a Christian as many in his congregation, let alone his seminarian classmates. He wasn't sure how long he could keep caddying for Jesus.

In Hot Water

Following golf the Monday after the Onion Sermon with Chris sitting in the right-hand seat, Jayne aimed the Miata toward East Crest Road and the lovely creek-side home she was renting. Inside she poured a mixture of iced tea and lemonade–an Arnold Palmer–for him and a South Australian shiraz for herself. Gazing through picture windows at the parade of mature Oaks marching from the creek up to the house and spa just outside, Chris said, "Another hidden jewel of Belle Waters. Do you keep your tub heated?"

"I do. Wanna sample it?"

The Reverend Christopher Hilding Ek did, she switched on the whirlpool, and after quickly stripping down to birthday suits, they wriggled in.

"Owiiieee! This is hot water!" he yelped, expecting the same comforting temperature he was used to from the pool at the health club.

"Interesting that you put it that way," she said with a devilish tone. "I've been picturing you in hot water for several days now." Chris sneezed a geyser of Arnold Palmer through his nose. Phlegm ran down his chest.

"You are contaminating this little bit of paradise," she said wiping him with a towel.

He felt so uncharacteristically relaxed and natural as he rat-a-tatted, "I only hope that I am not contaminating those other Edens: our golf course and church. But hey, my game was pretty good today, wasn't it? A forty-one with a ball out of bounds and two three putts. You should have conceded me that little one on nine. By the way, what did you wind up with? I was so frustrated with my closing double-bogie and the lost chance to break forty that I lost track of your score."

He smiled to himself as he thought "*Here we are like this and we're talking about golf. I like it. She is so good and natural for me. We're a couple.*"

"Thirty-seven. I was one over par for the nine."

"Good. Very good. Great." He said with little conviction. He was more interested in deconstructing his round than hers. "Seriously, Jayne, don't you think my golf game is improving? Keyshawn thinks so, or that's what he said when we last met out at his place."

"I guess it . . . is," she said drawing out the last two words as if to signal that she had more to say, but then deciding to keep quiet. Chris didn't respond so she added, "Is that what's bothering you these days? Your golf game?"

"Well, frankly yes," he said. "I take this so-called game very seriously, and I've got a sermon rattling around in my head that makes the case: Everyone should play their games as if they really count. For God's sake and for golf's sake? Right?"

She smiled back, but chose her words carefully after a long sip of wine. "Wellllll, I've been wondering if something else has been getting to you. You seem pre-occupied. Not your old self. What's up? It can't be just golf, can it?"

"Well, gimme a swig of that stuff and maybe my tongue will loosen up." he said, as he nudged closer to her and inhaled a couple of ounces of her red in one gulp. "Are you aware of the evaluation that the governing board did of me?"

"Well, no," she lied.

"I can't keep my mind off it." He paused. "My dear Ms. Nova, I am coming to the agonizing conclusion that I may not be in the job of my dreams. There's a lot of negative stuff dancing around me at Meadows. Get this: more than one or two people think I'm way too young to be a minister, and then they say I do very well leading the youth of the church. I can't tell who said what because of the way the anonymous answers were posted, but can't you see why I'm thinking about this a lot?"

She said, "They come from different people, don't they, the contradictory comments?"

"I suppose, but the whole thing has me wondering if I am in the right job or career or calling or whatever this gig is." The wine was having an effect.

"How long have you been feeling this way?"

"I don't know. Maybe I expect too much of myself, but do you realize how much I am supposed to do around here? For old people as well as the youth. Home visits, schmoozing, and when one of our members is doing something special like making a presentation at some organization or appearing before the city council or playing in the finals of a golf event or whatever else, I'm expected to be there. This must sound terrible me ranting on like this, but I feel I am at the point of, I don't know what? A change, I guess. What do you think?"

"Well, do you want me to be frank?"

"Of course." He took another draw on her wine.

"Well, okay, here's some psychoanalyzing, I think that your problems come from the youth of this church, not the old folks. I think you are threatened by Paige and her friends."

"Oh, come on. Don't be ridiculous."

"No, I mean it. I watch your reactions to their successes. The times the congregation lights up when they hit the nail on the head in talking about homelessness or when they knock them dead with a scriptural oration . . ."

". . . I could get jealous of *your* readings but not theirs."

". . . Hey, buddy. I hope I don't threaten you, except maybe on the golf course. *They* rattle your cage whether you admit it or not. I see it, but please understand this: *You* are given credit for it, and you should embrace it. When church members praise the youth, they are praising you. They may not say it at the time, but they value you. For good reason. You are a real find, and a gem. And not just to me. You are a successful minister."

Her phone, sitting on a lounge chair out of reach, rang.

". . . Hang on, I may have to take this one." With the smooth glide of a gymnast she pulled herself up the stairs out of the tub, picked up the phone, and walked into the house out of his hearing. Watching her smooth, wet body rise like a slow-motion porpoise, he was paying attention.

The phone conversation went on for fifteen minutes. When Jayne came back, she was in a long, maroon, terry cloth robe with a serious look on her face. "I'm really sorry, Chris, but I have to go. Something's come up. Please let's keep talking about this stuff. Your challenges. I think we should bring

Keyshawn into it. Not into my hot tub, though. That's just for the two of us. Okay?" She was trying to be funny.

They were silent for the most part as she drove him home and went to her office on campus. His head pounded.

Dual Roles

Most reasonable people would conclude that Chris was a fine human being and dedicated, talented young minister. He embodied behaviors that most parishioners value in each other and expect from their spiritual leaders. He recognized people's strengths, and told them in a graceful way. He listened, and hardly ever was thinking about the rejoinder he would spew when they paused. He didn't gossip and he was careful to avoid saying anything that could be construed as belittling somebody by damning them with faint praise. He was not a poseur or show-off. Without anybody ever knowing, he picked up litter and erased graffiti. He waved back at kids on school buses. He put–what for him were–big bills into the Salvation Army buckets at Christmas.

He liked it when good things happened to others. He got vicarious pleasure in their enjoyment. When his parishioners or friends outside the church went on trips to someplace he would love to visit, but never had, he got genuine pleasure learning about the high points and looking at their pictures. This was one admirable quality that Chris recognized in himself. Sometimes when alone he would make fun of himself, puff out his chest, and say out loud with a pompous BBC accent, "*I* am a vicar for the wonders of this world!"

But he was mainly self-critical. He saw himself–an ordained holy man–as self-centered and tentative. When he was a teenaged churchgoer, words from the pulpit said that everyone should be virtuous in thought, word, and deed. As an adult, he graded himself pretty high on word and deed, but until he took all those psychology courses, he wondered about his own thoughts. Aware of the silliness of controlling or revealing private thoughts, he smiled when he found out that former President Jimmy Carter had admitted–in a *Playboy* magazine interview of all places–that he had committed adultery in his thoughts. In his heart.

As a pastor with a flock, Chris was learning about his heart. He realized that he was walking across a stony meadow trying to balance the candor of his own beliefs with the gingerly presented messages that he delivered on Sunday morning. His professors and classmates at Chicago offered an answer: "Be true to your ordination vows required by our denomination, but feel free to have your own private thoughts as well. And don't necessarily feel guilty." But it wasn't easy.

Then came the relationship with Jayne, especially their increasing intimacies. Members had to know, or at least suspect, that he and she had something going. She wasn't a member of the church but acted like one, a fact that technically could help him duck conflict of interest charges if they became an issue.

Only lately had Chris seriously envisioned Jayne and him together for good. As a couple, like in engaged and then married. The issue brought worry along with teasing tingles. He had seen so many premature weddings turn into broken marriages. *"There's no need for people my age to rush to get married, is there? And living together indefinitely–in sin* (he smiled)–*just wouldn't work, even in a liberal congregation like Meadows."*

Jayne had so many attractive features. She was lively, forceful, and fun. She identified with organized religion in a way that respected it while holding back on reciting its–what she called overly Christian–creeds. She had plunged into Meadow's liturgical practices and was a force in its junior golf overture. She sang the hymns. She brought "dishes to pass" at church food fests. She contributed to Helping Hands while working to develop something deeper.

She marched to a different drummer than most members of Meadows, but never did she make fun of any of them, or gossip. But there was something about Jayne that was reserved and private. Chris could not see her as a member of the Discussion Group, because there was too much bearing of one's soul there. That's not this woman. Pastor Ek wished all members were as hard working and active as Jayne. She was a keeper as a churchgoer. As a wife? Yikes.

Project Newhomes

The Troublemakers met one more time to develop ideas from their earlier session. The goal: finish off a proposal about homelessness and send it to the governing board for their endorsement. Before they got down to business, Carleton quietly said, "Please, I want to share some things with you. Of course, you all know that I'm homeless–and so is Alan. Well I never–and I really mean never–talk about how I became homeless, but with you guys here and now, and considering what we're up to, I gotta say something. Do we have time? I'll make it brief."

Sharon and Alan didn't outwardly react. The others nodded. Chris was eager to hear details. When he first learned of Carleton's homelessness during their chance meeting at the confluence, he was full of questions, but he didn't feel the time was right to say "How did you get this way?" or "You don't seem like the homeless type." Or "Please tell me more." Up to this point in their brief relationship, Carleton had impressed Chris as a straight-talking, physically impressive man brimming with confidence. Tall and lithe. Healthy looking. Articulate in his directness. Chris saw him as somebody who was sensitive to the possibility that he–Carleton–could be intimidating to others and guarded against it with a slow soft voice. He listened and wanted to be heard. To be taken seriously. Now Carleton spoke quickly and his voice shook. He looked uncomfortable.

"What I'm going to say is just the tip of the iceberg. You can't really know what it's like to be homeless unless you've been there, and I'm not very good at sharing my feelings, but here goes. We're vets, Alan and me. Spent time working for Uncle Sam. Eight years. I enlisted in the army and felt so good about it then. During high school my family situation had gotten hopeless, I didn't have any plans to go to college and I wasn't employable. I needed to get away from the tension and fighting at home. I had–have–a brother who is two years older than me and was a star at school stuff. People called him a point of light or something like that. They still do. My 'parents' (He made quotation marks in the air with his finger)–actually my mother and her latest boyfriend–always compared me to him. Negatively. I couldn't do anything as well as he could. 'Why can't you be more like Bobby?' They would say snarly-like. It wore on me. Big time.

"So, that was one little hint of something that has to do with what I have become. Here's another: I liked electronic communications as a kid. I had a teacher who taught us to make crystal sets, you know, primitive radios. I thought they were magical. That guy–the teacher–was a ham radio operator. Do any of you know what that is? [Blank faces except for Jayne who gave a thumbs up]. Well, it's for amateur geek-types who like that sort of thing and like my teacher, I did. He got me started. A good guy. Now, the amateur radio that I assembled and used fifteen years or so ago, was hardly related to apps and websites and modern digital miracles, but my teacher said that if we know about the early origins of radio communications, we will be well prepared for learning new things. We'll understand them and feel their essence. That's how he put it. And army recruiters said something similar. So, when I enlisted I assumed that I would be able to learn all about modern communications and eventually, when I got out of the army, fall into a related job. Well, it turned out to be anything but that.

"Except for a little bit at the start, my three tours of duty overseas did not involve anything about electronics or radio. It was grunt work in Iraq where we spent countless hours doing nothing and then terrifying times riding from place to place on roads seeded with improvised explosive devices. IEDs. Roadside bombs. I cannot exaggerate how horrible they were or how scared we were just thinking of them. I get goose bumps just saying this now. The normal jarring of our trucks along rough roads could set them off as fireballs. I never got injured–physically–but three of my buddies were killed and others got burned.

"I was damaged by all that. I'm one of those posttraumatic effect statistics. I admit it, and I have tried to get help. I suppose that's part of the reason I'm homeless–the PTSD–but the main one is that I can't get hired. I am unprepared to do anything remotely related to what I thought I was going to learn when I enlisted. Like being trained to get a good job. And I have to share with you that I'm too proud to work at menial things. For a while I *thought* I was too proud to go back for help from my family–my mom and her latest 'friend'–but I tried. She was pretty nice to me for a while, but eventually things got intolerable for all of us, we got sucked up into tornado-like fights, and I left. I've been in Belle Waters for several months now. I've managed to find a few nights here and there from friends I met through Vet's Roll, that trip to Washington D.C. for veterans during Memorial weekend, but when I can, I camp along the river. Do you know that the number of homeless veterans today is greater than the number of soldiers who died during the Vietnam war?"

He stopped and everyone stayed quiet. Jayne, Chris, and Keyshawn tried to understand what Carleton was saying. Alan and Sharon felt it. Inside they were simmering. Glad that they were not telling their stories publicly like this.

But Alan had to add something. "You know, among homeless people golf has a funny little place. Some of the guys–I don't know about the women–scoff at golf. They think it's a snob's waste of time. Something to show off to the have not's. But others are fascinated by poor people who golf, like Carleton and me. They're curious about our attraction to the game. It's almost as if they are, well, envious of us because we golf. They think we are in a higher social status. Really. I tell them, we're all homeless, and so was our golfing hero, that Canadian Moe Norman."

Carleton jumped back in. "You know there is such a mix of people who are homeless. Some of them–us–were raised middle class. Others have been dirt poor all their lives. A few even come from families that are flat out rich. My point is don't ever stereotype us homeless as one group. We are diverse.

And golf. Well, like lots of lucky human beings, we get exposed to it and discover it's so challenging. The ecstasies that follow the agonies. The tugs at our muscles. The pals. You don't have to be rich to love golf. And just because we become homeless doesn't mean that we have to be golfless."

Al nodded.

Finally, looking at her watch, Paige said, "Thank you, Carleton and Alan," and they got down to the business of crafting what they wanted to emphasize in the proposal.

Sharon suggested lobbying state legislators to support a bill that would give more autonomy to younger homeless kids who are out on their own. Carleton and Alan made the case for a golfing component. Paige insisted on requiring all Meadows members to be members-in-more-than-name-only: To pledge in writing to host and mentor; to contribute time, in-kind help, and money; in short, to take membership seriously. Keyshawn was inspired by this forcefulness and took every opportunity to urge the others on. Jayne and Chris were quiet for the most part, gently pushing back and bringing up matters that they characterized as coming from devil's advocates.

The proposal presented to the Fair Are the Meadows Board was unanimously supported and signed by the Trouble Makers. It read as follows:

Reinforcing the Social Gospel of Fair Are the Meadows Church

Project Newhomes

Preamble

The timeless vision that guides what we propose here is our social gospel. "Social" means that we work together as we address our own needs and others'; "gospel" refers to Old and New Testament scriptures, plus centuries of reformed reactions to them.

The issue at hand is homelessness. At this point in our congregation's history a bold, confident, and widely embraced plan of action to combat homelessness can become a significant factor in whether we survive and flourish, or not. Making it happen requires that we are committed in word and deed.

Expected commitments of our members

Fair Are the Meadows Church of Belle Waters (FATM) commits to helping homeless young people get relief and grow in self-confidence. To this end, every member of our congregation will pledge to support the details of this proposal. *Rationale:* In addition to addressing a major message of the New Testament by helping others, our congregation will gain in fulfillment if we are 100% behind the effort.

Our church building will be expanded and redesigned to host homeless youth for negotiated lengths of time. *Rationale:* This gives a bricks and mortar signal that our commitment to Helping Hands is ongoing and expanding.

All members' homes will host homeless youth for negotiated lengths of time. *Rationale:* This gesture of generosity and vulnerability is a radical statement of our willingness to take the homeless dilemma seriously and to love our neighbors as ourselves.

All members will participate as mentors of homeless individuals. *Rationale:* Every one of us has gifts and talents that can be applied to helping others. As mentors, we bring these values to life.

Golf will be supported as a key in developing relationships between our members and the homeless. *Rationale:* While other means are possible, members must make every attempt to be part of the golfing culture that has become a force in our congregation's recent growth and renewed energy. Examples of participation include, but are not limited to: teaching the game to others; caddying; playing golf with our guests; accompanying guests to golfing competitions; developing writing projects about golf; depicting golf artistically; designing golf holes; building golf shelters; donating equipment (balls, clubs, bags, instructional videos); having more sermons about golf, along with any other way to make the most of this game that Pastor Chris has brought out of the shadows into the sunlight. We have basked in that light and must use it to help others and grow.

Our congregation will lobby the state of Wisconsin to pass a law that allows sixteen-year-olds to legally consent for their own admission to a shelter or transitional program for combatting homelessness. *Rationale:* Now they have to wait until they're eighteen, and yet most homeless kids, like those in the 16:49 program at the high school, are younger than that.

A Board of Advisors will provide input and feedback to the congregation regarding challenges, new possibilities, and successes. Every FATM member will be expected to serve on the Board. *Rationale:* The principles and procedures of our homelessness initiative need to be periodically reviewed and renewed. Ownership of this effort must be a commitment of every member.

Make what we value public. Share our vision widely and openly in the Stateline community and beyond. *Rationale:* We can be a unique, vibrant Christian congregation that appeals to many who have never heard of us, but in order for this to fully be realized, we must let them know who we are and what we do. God and golf.

Expected commitments of homeless guests

Share gifts and talents with members of FATM. Teach us something that you know and value. *Rationale:* We see all of our guests as persons with high potential. Learning is a two-way street. We must learn from them (you).

Learn about your FATM mentor(s). Find out their interests and future plans no matter how old your mentor is. *Rationale:* Establishing good human relationships is a two-way street.

Take your mentor to school events. *Rationale:* Familiarity and pride in one's educational environment promotes maturity and growth.

Accompany your mentor to a public event that is taking place in the Belle Waters area. *Rationale:* Learning about one's community promotes civic pride and ownership.

Contribute ideas to the Board of Advisors. Help FATM develop expectations for hosts and guests. *Rationale:* Ownership of the homeless project must extend to guests as well as hosts. Guests must be valued as full partners in the efforts. If the project is to succeed and grow, FATM must welcome the ideas of the guests.

Concluding Matters

We "Trouble Makers" fervently believe that this vision, if embraced, can give our congregation unity, dynamism, and hope. It can serve to keep our church family together based on a reinvigorated articulation of who we have been and who we seek to become. It can serve as a message to those who want to learn more about us, and join us: individuals, families, and/or congregations.

Pillow Talk

In bed the night after the Trouble Makers signed off on the final wording, Jayne said, "That proposal is so amateurish. What board would ever accept it?" She didn't say *our* proposal even though she signed her name along with all the others.

"They're just kids." Chis said.

"Not all of them. Not the golfers, including you."

"What didn't you like?"

"Well, so many things are left open or are truly unprecedented, and mark my words, members of this church won't let them go by. Like, what happens if some don't agree to participate? A lot will balk at taking in strangers, and think that the golf bit is beyond the pale? Asking all members to be golfers? You gotta be kidding. And preaching *more* sermons about golf. C'mon." She tickled him in the ribs.

"I thought you were a golfer," he said, starting to rub her neck.

"Oh, I play games of all sorts, but changing the subject, what about Paige? She's still out of control, and you let her get by with anything." Jane growled, "She's running the–what a stupid name–Trouble Makers like she runs everything else around here."

Chris said, "Hey, if we are going to keep talking, let's make it something pleasurable, like how about dem Cubbies?" Chris couldn't see her rolled eyes as he started to fake-snore. Soon they were both asleep.

Privately, Chris had worried about how the governing board and congregation would react to the homeless proposal. He knew the horror stories that tell about congregations who confront dicey issues and wind up tearing each other apart. Of course, he wondered how FATM's membership would support the demands of this proposal, but he didn't have the heart to go against what the Trouble Makers had created. He reminded himself that membership numbers were way up at FATM, youth participation was amazing, and feedback from the governing board regarding his ministry really was positive in spite of his gut-wrenching reactions to the negative criticism. He thought, "*Why* not *propose something ambitious and daring when the iron is hot. Bless the hearts of our kids, and these homeless treasures in our midst.*"

Proposal Presented Promptly

All the Trouble Makers arrived early at the scheduled seven p.m. governing board meeting ready to present, defend, and elaborate on the proposal. In fact, they were allowed to only speak briefly as part of an early agenda slot reserved for "congregational input." Paige led the charge. She introduced Sharon, Keyshawn, Alan, and Carleton, and then handed out hard copies of the proposal with a crisp overview and a smile: "This is something we have worked on body and soul. We support it unanimously. Please do the same. Pretty please?"

Then in an abrupt change of tone she closed with, "Seriously, if you do not accept this proposal–unanimously–we will not set foot in this church again. I mean it. Thank you."

The place went funeral home quiet with all eyes on Pastor Ek. He had a nano-second to decide how to react: either eyebrows arched with arms bent and palms up, or face down essentially looking at his shoes. He chose the latter.

Elder Stone broke the silence in a calm voice that Jayne later described as patronizingly polite. He thanked the Trouble Makers, but quickly added that the board had to get on with other business, and excused them with, "You may leave now unless you want to witness some boring stuff. It will be a long meeting, and we won't be discussing your proposal tonight."

Except for Chris, who stayed on in his role as pastor, they all left. Following Stone's directive, the board did not address the proposal that night, but before adjourning one member asked, "Just who are those people, I mean as a group. I'm sorry, I know them as individuals, but do I understand that they call themselves Troublemakers?"

Chris said, "Yep, but it's kind of in fun, the name."

"But, please, Pastor Ek, tell us about them . . ."

Stone intervened. ". . . we'll have plenty of time to react to this *in the future*. In the meantime, read it over and let's keep in touch. Share your reactions with everyone. That is, with the ten of us."

Pastor Chris added, "I think you should also copy the minutes of this meeting to the Trouble Makers."

The Future Arrives

The first electronic reaction to the proposal went out at 10:50 p.m. that night. Others followed so that by sunrise, six of the nine members of the board had responded:

> "What a great idea! These rock-solid members and our–is it polite to call them–homeless friends have knocked the ball out of the park. I love it! I'm with them!"

> "Tears came to my eyes as I took in the magnitude of what they are proposing. Demanding, actually. This group can be–is–our conscience and entrepreneurial spirit. I say let's go for it. Soon. It will make me feel like I deserve the benefits that come my way via Meadows."

> "What planet do these people come from? And what arrogance. Requiring. *Requiring*! members to take strangers into our homes? I'm pro-choice, not pro-chaos. It's no accident that no church that I have ever heard of does this. What about the safety and privacy of our families? Isn't the full name of our congregation Fair Are the Meadows *Family* Church? Am I supposed to put my family at risk, or at best dilute my time with them and support of them in caring for some people who obviously are troubled? I'm tempted to say some unwashed rabble, really, but even if they were squeaky-clean straight A students or hardworking employees, I'd object. Soooo, if I am asked to sign a

pledge to host strangers in my home, I have to say that I will no longer be a member of this church. Please realize that this is my initial reaction, and that I'm willing to listen to efforts that try to sell me on the goofy plan, but I can't imagine that I will come to support the hosting bit."

"I laughed hard when I first read the part about golf. Believe me, I really like that game, and I admit it has some subtle appeal that everyone might benefit from, but for a church to take on golf as a stated part of its mission? Whew! That's a heavy load. But, then I read the whole thing a second time and a third. The upshot: I think the golf piece could be a secret weapon in our quest for members and credibility. Kidding aside (not), churches have been built on squishier foundations: Sexism. Racism. Gerontocracy. Prosperity Gospel. Okay, with the exception of the Prosperity Gospel these are not values that are openly bragged about, but they are powerful forces that truly have governed actions. We would be advertising our golfing culture as a friendly force, and we'd work hard to make mentors disciples. We could call them Caddies for Jesus (Ha ha!). It's very late at night and I'm typing this much faster than I usually do, but I am totally serious: this proposal looks promising, and I would vote for it as is right now. P.S. I have heard that there are congregations that base their existence on the foundations of football (Soccer), anti-colonialism, euthanasia, the physical healing powers of faith, pub culture, and satan [Please note that I am not capitalizing the name for this devil]. And I know there are lots of them out there that believe in a human being who becomes God."

"If anything, this church needs to become more political. Not in a partisan sense like we're Democrats or Republicans, but in explicitly supporting (or opposing) emerging laws. I know for a fact that many totally capable Belle Waters teen-agers younger than the legal age of eighteen are homeless but unable to consent to their own admission into shelters or transitional homes like the ones being proposed here. Kids can be amazing. Look at ours here at Meadows. Thanks, Pastor Chris. And a big thanks goes to our Paige and may I say *our* Sharon?"

"So, for discussion's sake, let's say I don't want to be a mentor. I want to learn from and contribute to this church. I want to give my money and time, but I want some choice in the activities that I participate in. Why should I be forced to do something that is out of my comfort range? I really like Meadows and I enjoy serving on the governing board for the most part, but isn't this place tolerant of various ways of contributing? We say we are. Wouldn't following the letter of this proposal force us into a narrow new ministry? I see it chasing away members like me. Sorry. And I wouldn't be true to myself without saying that Paige is a pain in the you know where."

Crisis and Confession

Paige texted Chris as soon as she got home. "I need to talk. I really regret what I said at the meeting tonight. How about early tomorrow at your office?"

"Of course, I'll be there by . . . is seven okay?"

Paige tapped gently on the door. When Chris opened it, she sobbed uncontrollably and fell into his arms. He gave her a handful of tissues, and they sat down side by side on a sofa. She began,

"I was out of control last night. What I said at the end about not coming back may be true for me, but I can't speak for everyone. We never mentioned what we would do if we lose, and how could I be so self-centered that I thought I could speak for everyone and they'd just fall in line? But you know what, Chris? What makes me so sad? It's that I mean it. I can't come back here if they turn this down, and early reactions look like they might. Might not make it unanimous, and that's what I have to have. Is it unreasonable for us to require those changes? To make our members become real doers for the religion that we all profess is so true and good? To *make* them do it? To shake them out of their luke warm beliefs? Don't they have to pledge to do things to be members of this church, like act out creeds, or something? Kids have to when they become confirmed. "I want them to take their religion seriously! I do–take it seriously–don't I? Take it seriously?"

She looked him in the eye. "Am I missing something, Chis–Pastor Chris–my rock-steady guide and father-confessor?" She stopped talking and sobbed quietly.

Chris, like Paige, was nervous at the start of their conversation, but the more she talked the more relaxed he became. And clear-headed. He stayed still for what seemed like a long time after her opening salvo, and didn't answer her questions directly, getting his thoughts together. Then he said,

"Okay, here's how I see it: People understand things differently. There may be–is–a world out there that seems to be the same for all of us, but we don't take it in the same. I know some who think that leadership of a church means getting members to fall into line, but I'm certainly not one to sing that tune. I'm no literalist and, sadly, I suppose, I'm no leader. I learned long ago to try to see things from the point of view of others and I probably go too far in that direction. So, if I were reading the proposal for the first time, objectively, I very likely would say it *demands* too much."

"Why didn't you say that during our planning meetings?"

"I thought I did, but you and–I guess–the others didn't want to hear it. Leading a church is not easy. For the pastors, especially the young ones like me, everyone is your boss. Okay, that's not fair for me to say about Meadows. Here everyone is your well-meaning mentor, but there are conflicting lobbyists out there. A few want me to clearly lay it out in no uncertain terms; others say I should stay in the background and pull the right strings. Jayne says it's the tension between being a sage on the stage or a guide on the side. I guess I'm a guide."

Paige showed a little smile, and said, "Duh, no kidding," while wiping her eyes.

"You know, Paige, I have sometimes shared my own insecurities with you and the other kids. Usually, I regret it at first, but then realize, why not? I want you to know me as I am, not as some role-player. I rationalize my fence-riding or submission to the will of the congregation by thinking that as a minister I must be true to my denomination and the people in the pews even if it clashes with who I really am. For example, a church has to have a balanced budget over time, and it better be growing. The membership. Sometimes if members don't get what they want, they threaten to leave. Once in a while they do. And while we are often thought of as a liberal congregation, there are many values out there some of which could be thought of as conservative . . .

". . . like what?"

". . . well, I'd say maybe balancing a budget, having a clean sanctuary, providing music that comes from way back in our tradition, thinking before acting, showing discipline in our individual behavior as well as a flock, etc. Okay? Enough? Anyway, dear Paige, whatever label we may like or have foisted upon us, we must be flexible and not demand. We need members. We need pledges. We need reasonable guidelines. A lot of what that proposal says–demands–is way too much."

Paige got up and left. Chris waited for the door to be slammed, but she shut it gently.

The Ayes Have It

Word got out that the board voted 5 to 4 in favor of the proposal. The congregation was confused on what this would mean. Tongues wagged. The powers that be had to set things straight. These words came from on high.

"A Letter to the Congregation of Fair Are the Meadows Church

From Eberhard Stone, Chair of the Governing board

"Dear Friends in Christ:

"We assume that most of you have already learned that a very ambitious and heartfelt overture regarding homelessness has been presented to us, your governing board. It is called Reinforcing the Social Gospel of Fair Are the Meadows Church. I have attached a copy here and you can read it on our church website.

"The proposal came from a group of dedicated members and friends of Meadows who call themselves 'Trouble Makers.' I like that name. I have always thought of myself as a trouble maker, in the best sense of course.

"Our board initially favored the proposal as written. Not unanimously, but there were more supporting than opposing: 5 ayes to 4 nays.

"In some groups and institutions even such a narrow margin means that a decision has been made and should be acted on, because one side prevailed. So, everyone should honor the decision, pull together, and move ahead. Many laws and court decisions are determined like this in secular society, and the same thing happens from time to time in religious governance.

"But sometimes more than a mere majority of votes is desirable when confronting issues that involve significant change: A 'strong majority' is needed. This may be invoked to make sure that a sizable proportion of voters are ready. So, they don't jump into things prematurely. So, they know what they are doing. So, tradition is honored and not thoughtlessly cast aside.

"Those of us on the board have prayed and discussed this proposal and decided not to move ahead with it in spite of our early vote. We feel that Meadows would need a very strong majority for this proposal to succeed, to really be put into action.

"Several particular–they called them–demands caused us concern. All would be very difficult to implement. Please read the precise wording from the proposal but I summarize them here as follows: significant fund-raising in addition to what we are already doing, violation of the sanctity of our homes, golf for everyone, lobbying of elected officials, a non-member board that would direct us, and full support of all details.

"Now, each of these points if taken on its own is pretty darned significant if you ask me and not bad. Probably good. Taken as a package, and that's what those troublemakers are requiring, it's overwhelming. While our board members who voted in favor of it–five of them, us–were convinced by the argument that we should do something big, upon sober reflection we slowed down and got our feet on the ground. Reconsidering our original vote, we unanimously decided to table the proposal.

"Let me make this next point perfectly clear: We unanimously appreciate what the Trouble Makers have done: the time, creativity, and passion in their overture. They are treasures in our midst but we have to consider and protect the traditions and cohesion of our congregation. We cannot invite dissention and division. We must stay together.

"Finally, we are willing to talk more with our trouble-making friends while remembering that compromise is not a bad word. Here's the main point: We have lots of differing opinions in our congregation and we want everyone to be content. To feel good about this wonderful church.

"Yours faithfully,

"Ebby Stone"

Paige was heartbroken. Jayne was angry. Keyshawn, Alan, Carleton, and Sharon were disappointed. Pastor Chris was not surprised. To himself he had predicted the vote would be 6 to 3, perhaps a workable beginning for some tangible progress in a revised proposal. The day after Stone's message went out, Paige replied on the church website:

"To the Congregation of Meadows Church

"From Paige Ahlgren

"About the future

"I am disappointed about the vote of the administrative committee. Actually, I'm heart-broken, and while I have great affection for this congregation and its many members–friends–I feel deflated and out of energy.

"I've asked myself, what is a church mainly for? Is it community with mutual support of members? Sure. Is it taking risks in following the lead of Jesus? I'm not so sure. I have made fun of those bumper stickers whose acronym asks What Would Jesus Do? And I know that many in our contemporary society behave as if that's irrelevant–he's irrelevant–but it gets to me. The question. I think it's a legitimate one if–and this is a huge if–we take our membership and mission seriously. The scripture is full of guidance. I hear these words:

"Isa 58:7 Is it not to share your bread with the hungry and bring the homeless poor into your house . . .?

"Luke 3:10-11 And the crowds asked him, "What then shall we do?" And he answered them, "Whoever has two tunics is to share with him who has none, and whoever has food is to do likewise."

"Matt 7:12 "So whatever you wish that others would do to you, do also to them, for this is the law . . ."

"I have tried to take Christian stories seriously. The ones we hear from our pulpit and read from our Bibles talk about Jesus and his parents as homeless. As people who were taken in. I heard them early–the stories–told by my mother in Sunday school but also at home. I know they have made her a hard worker who tries to do good.

"So, what has that made me? A self-centered juvenile? A person lacking in social graces who doesn't know when to quit? A dreamer? I'll let others decide and I'm not sure where I am going in the future. Probably not the ministry, but who knows? (That's supposed to be funny).

"No matter what this congregation decides about some compromised version of our proposal, or not, I hope that you open your eyes to the homelessness surrounding you in this town and everywhere. Please, I beg of you, *empathize* with the hopelessness, disruption, stress, worry and danger of being without a home. Please–in one way or another–listen to homeless people. Provide mentors and role models for them. Support efforts outside of Meadows to help them. Love them. Give them a voice. Expect them to teach you. Take a chance on your best angels. Keep working with Helping Hands, but do something daring as well.

"In faith,

"Paige Ahlgren

After the letter from Mr. Stone, none of the Trouble Makers attended services at Meadows for a long time except for Keyshawn Gentry, who had become a regular on Sunday mornings.

11

Commencement

Me and LBJ

SIX MONTHS AFTER THAT first dip into Jayne's hot tub and two months after the Trouble Makers presented their plan to the governing board, Chris preached a sermon he publicly entitled The Next Shot. To himself he referred to it as Me and LBJ.

Lyndon Baines Johnson was President of the United States in 1968, an election year. On March 30, he gave what was billed an important speech about the war in Vietnam. For a long time that evening the nation heard him drawl on about the agonies of conflict, the sacrifices of thousands, and the lives lost. He called out the political adversaries who criticize the Commanders-in-Chief who make the big decisions and must live with them. He talked about gains that must not be lost in suspicion, distrust, and selfishness in politics. He said, "I have concluded that I should not permit the Presidency to become involved in the partisan divisions that are developing." Then in the last couple of minutes of the homily, he spoke the words that shocked everyone and changed America.

In his The Next Shot (Me and LBJ) sermon, Pastor Ek looked down at his notes and recited advice he had received from his golf teacher Keyshawn Gentry: "Your next shot is the most important one you will ever take. You can't do anything about those flaws of the past, so try to make the future shine. Concentrate. Bring together all of your resources to hit your *next* shot squarely. Don't let mistakes of the past get to you. Think. Plan. Execute and overcome. Do it right away. Hop up and ride that horse that threw ya."

Gentry was trying to lead his students beyond traumas like the destroyed hopes coming from a triple bogie early in their round, or an out-of-bounds shot or shank moments ago: their *last* shot. So, the next shot becomes critical.

Pastor Ek carried his golf bag to the front of the sanctuary at the beginning of the service and plopped it down at a prominent spot next to the pulpit. After sharing Mr. Gentry's wisdom, he pulled out a seven iron and took his stance. He waggled the club head and wiggled his behind. He was a golfer about to take a swing at an imaginary ball. All of this up front in the nave of Fair Are the Meadows church.

As his club raced through the hitting area, he shouted out the sound that comes from a solidly hit shot– thu *weck*!–and said, "That makes me feel so good!" as he assumed the exaggerated high-hands follow-through of a satisfied golfer watching his ball's parabolic arc bisecting a fairway. Then he turned, looked out at the gallery of smiling faces in the pews and said, "I think I'll hit another one. Okay?"

"Yesss," was the emphatic reply.

This one didn't go well. It was that ugliest of outcomes when the club imperfectly meets the ball: the diabolical shank. Or in the cleaned-up language of Harvey Penick, a lateral shot.

"Fore! Duck!" he yelled during his awkward follow through, and acted as if the ball was heading right at the people. They played their roles and took cover.

"Sorry about that," he said, "but you should be sorry for me, or at least empathetic. The hardest shot in golf is the one right after a shank like that, and you have no choice whether you are going to swing again right away. You must." Then he talked about getting right back on a bicycle after falling off, about apologizing right after doing something stupid, and about studying hard right away after–he called it–screwing up a test that you didn't take seriously. About starting over right away in the wake of a bad scene.

"All of us can diminish the effects of a bad golf shot by following the advice of this man I call *Professor* Gentry and I am going to try to build the case this morning that it applies to more important parts of our lives as well." Keyshawn Gentry was out there in the pews. The pastor pointed at him and winked. Then paraphrasing from what Gentry had once preached, Ek said that the past can be one of our worst enemies when trying to make a fresh start. And he read from his Bible.

"Isa 43:18-19. "Remember not the former things, nor consider the things of old. Behold, I am doing a new thing; now it springs forth, do you not perceive it? I will make a way in the wilderness and rivers in the desert.

"Phil 3:13-14. Brothers and sisters, I do not consider myself yet to have taken hold of it. But one thing I do: Forgetting what is behind and straining toward what is ahead, I press on toward the goal to win the prize for which God has called me heavenward in Christ Jesus.

"Rev 21:4. And God shall wipe away all tears from their eyes; and there shall be no more death, neither sorrow, nor crying, neither shall there be any more pain: for the former things are passed away.

Then he spoke at length about the traditional interpretations of each of the selections and their places in the Christian story. In drawing the sermon to a close he emphasized the timeliness of–what he called–these precious words.

Pastor Ek had leaned his seven iron against the pulpit. Now he picked it up–lovingly, Gentry would later say–and looked like he was going to hit another ball, but first he went back to talking about LBJ. Slowly with emphasis on every word and a tiny Texas twang, he said that at the end of his 1968 speech Lyndon Baines Johnson said, "I shall not seek and I will not accept the nomination of my party as your President." Words that changed so much: He would not run for re-election. He would not continue to be leader of the free world.

Ek paused, and then said in closing his sermon, "Similarly, my dear friends, I will not be continuing as your pastor. My decision has been made. It is final. You have just heard my last sermon in this holy place."

Then with the congregation looking on in stunned silence, he hit another shot. Based on his body language, it went straight and pure. He didn't go to the back of the sanctuary for the usual receiving line, but exited from a door at the front, went into his office, and shut the door.

The Solipsist Faints

Postings on the church Facebook page came quickly. The first one struck Pastor in the gut when he logged in on Sunday afternoon:

> "We at Meadows have just experienced the most self-centered, solipsist sermon in the history of Christendom. Is Ek the only sentient being walking these parts? To compare himself with LBJ would be laughable were it not so tied to the future of this congregation. We–Meadows–need to be a place of spiritual security and predictability, not a psychoanalyst's couch for–what does he sometimes call himself–a searcher? I'm boiling mad so I may regret these words later, but I say good riddance."

Chris fainted when he read it. He came to sweating and short of breath with his heart pounding and blood pressure spiked to the sky. Fortunately, he went again to his screen right away–hopped back on that horse–read the next post, and began the ascension from way down below. It said,

"I love Pastor Chris. I always will even if he never sets foot in our church again. He has taught me–us–so much, but what I like the most is that he gives us a chance to see into what makes him tick. Today's sermon was classic Chris and the best one I have ever heard. It had everything: drama, laughter, history, participation–we all ducked when that ball shanked off his club–but most of all he gives us candor. I appreciate clergy who level with us poor slobs out in the pews, about their own state of mind as well as what they are taught at seminary and what they say when they are with their old buddies over a beer. If I have a minister who is conflicted about his own faith or future, I want to know. Okay, people will say TMI–too much information–and I suppose somebody can go too far in sharing their own struggles. People would rather be led by somebody steadfast, confident, and strong–but, duh, aren't ministers human? And wasn't Jesus human (I think Jesus was sexually active, but I have only said that in private to a few confidants until now, but why wouldn't he be? And why should we be afraid to speculate about it, but I'm wandering *and* trying to be candid.). Chris has been the best thing in the world for our kids. I'm not one of them, but a kid at heart I hope. They are the lay leaders of this church these days. They are willing to take chances. They listen. Really, they do. *Listen to them!* Now I am getting preachy, but my main message here is a huge thank you to Pastor Chris. I want to know more about your plans and hopes, but you have already left a mark on this congregation that can propel us into a fine future."

The number of postings grew that day and into the week. Most of them were short and positive. Some were perfunctory and obligatory. Several asked if he was leaving because of the "failure" of the homelessness project. Many asked for details about his own plans: What's next for you? How do you see us moving on? How much longer will you be around? Some had memorable words and passages. *Jewels,* Chris thought as he first read them, but thought again. *Costume* jewelry? Do they really mean these words?

"Aren't we all ministers of one kind or another?"

"Chris! Will you still be willing to give me advice on how to get rid of my shank–when you are out of here?"

"We have not appreciated you, but do you appreciate us?"

"Hey, what's up with you and that Jayne Nova fox?"

"You grip the lectern too tightly."

"Have you ever thought of getting a dog?"

Back to the Teacher

Chris stayed scarce after the LBJ sermon. He cancelled his usual Monday morning golf game with Jayne, didn't respond to messages, and didn't go outside, but he made one outgoing call. To Keyshawn about getting together Monday afternoon. It happened. They talked and walked along the river.

Gentry began with, "My good pastor, you are so kind. You mentioned me yesterday from the pulpit. I ducked down with the rest of them when your shank came at us, and I really liked your follow-through on the last shot you hit. You're starting to get this game of golf. Right?"

Chris didn't respond.

His teacher continued, "Seriously, though, I heard you yesterday, man, and I think I know where you're coming from. Do you want to talk about that, or anything? *You* called *me*."

"Where to begin," Chris said and paused. Fifty yards later he began, "Here's the heart of it: I know so little and don't do much. I'm not ready to be a spiritual guide for others. There's a lot more wisdom out in our pews than up in the pulpit when I'm there. Mark Twain said one sign of achieving maturity is when you get old you realize how little you know and how much others do. Well, I must be old in spite of the fact that some of our members think I'm so young. But I don't have wisdom."

He wasn't fishing. It was from the heart.

"You do."

"No, I don't. Some of the kids in my youth class are better Christians than I am."

"So what," Gentry said.

The pastor said, "What do you mean?"

On the phone Chris had told Keyshawn about that first posting after the LBJ sermon and how he had passed out. He also described the positive tributes that followed, but the brutal words that Chris would always remember as "that solipsist message" were hard wired into his brain: self-centered, laughable, good riddance. And he shared with Keyshawn the fact that he actually felt good about the "defeat" of the proposal.

"Well, I'm certainly not going to take back my resignation. I'm finished at Meadows and I know that's for the best for the church and for me."

"But in your sermon on Sunday didn't you say that when we experience something negative we should respond positively right away? I liked your golf examples."

"You should, you taught them to me."

"Well?"

"Look, Keyshawn. We say that golf and life overlap, but that's exaggerated."

"No kidding."

"Seriously, you know that I really like golf. Okay, I love it, but the comparisons of the agonies and ecstasies of life with golf are way overdrawn. I've given too many sermons about golf, and I've let our church become too linked to the game. It's one of my regrets, but not the big one."

"And just what is that?"

"I don't know where I am headed, and so how can I lead others? You know, there are people in this congregation–of all ages–who are more Christian than I am, but maybe even more importantly, there are people who get things done better than I do."

"Who?"

"Oh, c'mon PGA golf pro Keyshawn Gentry: Joyce, Paige, Ebby. I could go on."

Keyshawn Gentry said, "Mr. Stone? Are you serious?"

"Yes. He knows what he wants and goes after it. I get all introspective and soul baring. You see, one reason the solipsist posting got to me is that it's hitting the mark. I do think too much of myself. Maybe everyone does–I suppose even Joyce Ahlgren does–but they help others along the way. More and more I'm wrapped up in how I am doing and what others are thinking of me and the impact that I will have on others and what is best for me without really *doing* anything. I think I'm afraid to really put my heart and soul totally into something. Jayne says I have a fear of success."

"You're being too hard on yourself."

"I don't think so."

Gentry was a listener for much of the rest of their walk. Ek confided that he might have chosen the ministry impulsively without realizing all that was involved. He blamed the seminary for some of it–Why didn't they tell us more about the unresolved issues?–but kept hammering away at himself. He said he wished he were twenty years older, like those so-called mature seminarians coming out of the woodwork who have lived a lot of life before going into the business of serving as a role model for others. At this point Keyshawn pointed out that Jesus was a very young man.

Chris shot back that he wasn't Jesus in any way, shape, or form. Nobody is. Well, hardly. He added that there are such folks–he calls them Christ-like –out there and maybe they should be the shepherds of the sheep. Then he said that he didn't like that metaphor. Church members should be thoughtful independent developing souls, not automatons. When he said this, Gentry interrupted.

"Look, Chris. Your members are thoughtful, and although they don't necessarily follow your every lead, they have shown themselves to be sensitive to many things you have encouraged. The youth of this church are on fire. You took them seriously and they responded."

Into Chris's head flew that line from Handel's *Messiah* that inspires him each Christmas: *He is like a refiner's fire.*

Filling Out an Application

It asked, "Tell us about your qualifications and why you want to be a Volunteer."

Chris's first draft included the following:

". . . I've been called a solipsist. You know, somebody who has an extreme preoccupation with their own feelings and thoughts. I wouldn't call myself that, but I'm trying to understand how others might . . . do. I am a youngish (28 years old) ordained United Church of Christ minister who is grappling with a need to be more candid with himself and his parishioners, and in the process, I may be projecting from the pulpit somebody who is self-absorbed. That solipsist bit hurts, but I am willing to put up with it if I can make progress on other fronts like those describing the goals of the Peace Corps: promoting world peace and friendship, helping countries and communities be all that they can be, etc. . Corny? Overstated? Maybe, but I have those goals myself and while they have been partly realized by my first ministerial call in Belle Waters, Wisconsin, I need more and Lord only knows there's a need.

"I doubt whether you get many responses like mine, but I am trying to build a case that presents me as a potential contributing Peace Corps Volunteer. And I'm trying to level with you. Tell the truth as I understand it.

"Many members from my congregation think that I have had great success motivating youngsters. It is a fact that the youth of our church have energized the whole place. Some say *they*–these fledgling teenagers–have become the guiding soul of the church (It's called Fair Are the Meadows Family Church) and that *I* have been the reason for their amazing transformation from typical apathetic teens preparing for confirmation to bundles of energy committed to the future of–we shorten it to–Meadows. (Do you know how to get bats out of a church belfry? Confirm them. They'll never come back.) On a smaller scale when I was in seminary I had success with disaffected youth at a struggling church in Chicago, so I have acquired a reputation as somebody who can get through to youth.

"Here's the problem: I don't fully understand how I am carrying it out or not, and they–the kids–are *doing* things while I'm mainly just talking about it or out playing golf. I have used my passion for golf as a way to get through to people and to show them what makes me tick. The point is this: I need to do something. Minimize the words. Keep the golf–I'll never give that up–but get my hands dirty. Obviously, I am self-centered, but my favorite philosophy professor in college said everyone is *by nature self-centered*. He emphasized those words, but added that how we proceed to realize our–he called them–fully functioning selves can be utterly altruistic.

"I have examined possible openings in the Corps and the one that says Secondary English Teacher in Durban, South Africa, especially appeals to me. I have followed golf in that country. They have had some stellar white players, but they also have an untold story that I want to–let's say–exploit as I teach children English. It's about Sewsunker 'Papwa' Sewgolum, a South African of Indian descent whose talent and persistence decades ago came through in the face of the discriminatory sports codes of apartheid. Papwa's story is similar to ones that I have encountered among African-Americans who take to golf, building on their experiences as caddies. In my church ministry, I have tried to combine the inherent attractions of golf with larger values while sharing tales of those who have overcome bias and exclusion. There are a lot of caddies at Meadows . . ."

Jayne's Take

Chris attached the draft application as a pdf in an email to Jayne. Upon first reading she laughed out loud. At it. She whipped back a response that said,

"You have got to be kidding. Are you serious here? Do you think the Peace Corps would do anything but stuff this and the rest of your application into their electronic shredder? Golf and national service? Golf in South Africa amongst anyone but the rich whites who still rule there in many ways? C'mon. You are cheeky and overly casual in how you put this together, and you haven't developed the power of your case. I recommend a complete rewrite. Do you want me to help? P. S. I love you."

The Students' Take

On the Sunday afternoon following the Me & LBJ revelation Gloria texted the others with a message that had the subject line: We gotta meet about Pastor Chris! She said, "How about getting together before school Tuesday? Everybody came and gathered in the Riley Room. Everybody except

Paige raved about their fella: "He's the best . . . a listener . . . fun to be with
. . . our advocate . . . a good sport . . . humorous . . . willing to laugh at
himself . . . a true Christian . . . a fine teacher and preacher . . . a learner . . .
What are we going to do without him? . . . He could be a wonderful Peace
Corps Volunteer."

Paige waited until they all had their say. After an awkward silence with
everyone looking at her, eyes down she said, "Oh, he's fine. Not bad at all,
but let's be careful not to exaggerate."

"What do you mean?" Pauline said.

"Well, you all act like he's God's gift to I-don't-know-what, but I've
seen him in some situations where he was baffled and intimidated . . ." She
stopped and looked up.

Beverly said, "Please say more."

Paige gave her impressions of Chris when he and she met with the
governing board that first time, another when he was with her and Joyce,
and several descriptions of how he impressed her (not) on the golf course.
The kids were squirming. They respected Paige's point of view, and let her go
on without interrupting, but she was a minority of one and unlike with Lincoln, here the majority prevailed. Led by Gloria, they started to talk about a
Sunday at Meadows where they would take charge of everything–sermon,
liturgy, a lunch afterward, and a chance to give gifts in honor of Pastor Ek's
time with them. Of course, he would have to be there, and one way or another they would squeeze some words from him about his future. Public
comments. Not the gossip that has already started.

Paige said, "Did you hear what Stone is saying? That Ek and Nova are
joining the Peace Corps as a couple."

They tried to create a Sunday service, the kids, but floundered with
the devilish details and decided instead to plan a funeral service for their
minister. It unfolded like a crisp new score card at the beginning of a round
of golf on a sunny May morning.

I love you

Chris read over Jayne's reaction to his Peace Corps qualifications draft so
many times he could recite it from memory, but everything–her focus, objectivity, and clear-headedness–faded compared to the last three words. He
dwelt on the fact that she didn't say "Luv ya," or 'Ta Luv,' or 'Lots of Love,'
or some other affectionate throwaway. Could she possibly mean it? What
difference would it make if she did? He had been thinking along these lines
himself, but never came close to letting on in so many words.

Maybe she sensed something from him that caused her to take the voiced leap. He was glad she said it first, but was it because he was too lacking in pluck to move on or too fearful to be rejected? He thought he could marry her and then the two of them go off to some Peace Corps assignment together. It wouldn't be the first time a Belle Waters clergyman and his wife did that. He also thought of them committing to each other in some sort of bond that would be even better than marriage, while they lived apart with Skype and occasional visits to keep them fresh. He in South Africa. She in who knows where. And he thought of cutting it off with her altogether. *"It's insane: Of course, we're not ready for marriage considering how little we know about each other. It would hurt to lose her. She could be my first love, I sometimes think, but did she mean it? Would I if I gave the usual response?"*

He didn't change a word of his application.

The Funeral Service

In her opening comments to the more than 200 people in the sanctuary celebrating their pastor's tenure at Fair Are the Meadows Church, Gloria, speaking for the youth, said, "We know that Pastor Chris likes living obituaries–funeral services, actually–that are held before the big day when we say goodbye forever, so here is our attempt to give him one. He didn't talk much about real death with us in our class, but it was waiting in the wings and worked its way into some of the literature that he shared like in 'I have promises to keep and miles to go before I sleep.' So, with that theme for starters, I'm going to ask Pauline to get specific as we contemplate Death and Pastor Ek."

She began, "After a particularly inspiring worship service a member of Meadows–who will not be named here–greeted Pastor Ek at the back of the sanctuary and said, 'That was a wonderful sermon. You should have it published.'

"Our proud pastor puffed up and replied, 'Actually, I'm planning to have all my sermons published posthumously.'

"'Great,' gushed the member. 'The sooner the better.'"

A few groans morphed into a sprinkle of laughter that grew. Chris smiled, shook his head from side to side, and got red in the face. Pauline continued,

"Not really, Pastor Chris, . . . that death wish for you. We want you to live a long, tasty life, but you do tell us that time goes so fast that forever is right around the corner and we better be prepared. Right?"

The Reverend Christopher Hilding Ek–sitting up front in a big beat-up arm chair that had been moved from his office and that here acted as a throne–raised his hands high and shouted "Yessss!"

Everyone clapped.

Gloria moved things along. "Our man here always stresses that we have to pitch in and work hard. The next commentary is called Working with God to be read by Henry." He began,

"A farmer in rural Belle Waters, who used to attend Meadows church, purchased an old abandoned spread with plans to turn it into a thriving enterprise. The fields were overgrown with weeds, the barn was falling apart, and the fences were collapsing. During his first week as pastor of our church, Reverend Ek drove out there with the objective of softening him up in order to ultimately bring him back into our pews. After awkward small talk that wasn't getting anywhere, he blessed the man's work by saying, 'May you and God work together to make this the farm of your dreams. And he left.

"A few months later Pastor stopped by again to call on the farmer. Lo and behold, it was a completely different place. The barn was in excellent condition, there were cattle and pigs devouring feed in well-fenced areas, and the fields were planted with healthy crops in neat rows.

"'Amazing!' Chris exclaimed. 'Look what God and you have accomplished together!'

"'Yes, Reverend, but remember what the farm was like when God was working alone.'"

The congregation loved it and so did Chris. He called out so everyone could hear, "If a parsley farmer is sued, can they garnish his wages?" Everyone groaned. Chris said, "That's from a former member of Meadows who now lives in Virginia. Emil Kreider. He sends me things like that."

"It figures. That had Kreider all over it." Jerry Geneva said to Jan out in the pews, cupping his hand over his mouth, but everyone around them could hear.

Next Gloria said, "We all know how finances and human relations are a part of any vocation, including the ministry. Ordained leaders must be stewards of a church's treasure while nurturing its staff. They also must have a sharp eye for talent and hire the best people for jobs that come vacant. With this in mind, the search committee and church board that hired Pastor Chris certainly deserve our thanks, but so does Chris for his role in the recent hiring of our new organist. In case you aren't aware of how it all happened, here's Jimmy to tell you."

"Pastor Ek was preoccupied with thoughts of how he was going to ask the congregation to come up with more money than was anticipated for repairs to our building. Consequently, he was annoyed when he learned that our soon-to-retire organist was ill and that a substitute had to be brought in at the last minute. Naturally, the sub wanted to know what music to perform.

"'Here's a copy of the what I have chosen for the service,' Pastor Ek said. 'But, you'll have to think of something on your own to play after I make a sobering announcement about the finances of Meadows church.'

"Late in the service Pastor made his pitch. It closed with the words, 'Brothers and sisters. We are in great difficulty. The roof repairs cost twice as much as we expected and we need $4,000 more. Any of you who can pledge at least $100, please stand up.'

"At that moment, the organist played the Star-Spangled Banner, and that is how the substitute organist became the regular organist."

They loved it. Hooting, clapping, and making Mary-Beth, the new organist, take a bow.

Gloria moved on. "I think we all have gotten the message that Pastor Chris likes feedback. He especially delights in meeting and glad-handing us at the back of the sanctuary after his sermons, but when somebody comments on the substance–the meat of his message–he is in heaven. But (sigh) it doesn't always happen that way.

"The Sunday morning I am describing had ended and Pastor Chris was greeting us as we were leaving. Everyone was friendly, but no one said anything about the sermon. He was getting a little concerned about that until one of you–I won't name names–said, 'Oh, Pastor, your sermon reminded me of the peace and love of God.'

"Pleased with the gesture but a bit puzzled since he didn't necessarily intend that message as a focus for the morning, Chris asked her to explain what she meant. She said, 'Well, that sermon was about the peace of God because it passed all understanding, and it reminded me of the love of God because it endured forever.'"

Chris began clapping. Everyone joined in. Then he said, "Thanks, I needed that."

Gloria thought, "*What a guy.*"

Paige thought, "*So true.*"

Ebby thought, "*What a show boat,*" as he strolled to the front and with the presence and authority of his office said, "Aren't these kids great? Let's give *them* a big hand." And that happened. Then he added, "But we haven't finished hearing reactions to Pastor Ek's life with us. Super Secretary Sandy, c'mon up here and give us your take on this guy."

Sandy hadn't been at the church recently due to her leave of absence and wondered how she would be received since the scuttlebutt was that things weren't getting done as well now as when she was on the job. Her quick departure was not appreciated. But an extended round of applause along with hoots and whistles told her that they still loved her.

She said, "Thank you. Thank you, dear friends," and then got down to business. "Now, about our departing leader: I was taught by a venerable past minister of this church that there are three key questions to ask if you want to find out how a minister is doing. Here they are. Think Chris.

"Does he make the congregation laugh, and doesn't just saying his name make you at least smile?" She leaned toward the assembly cupping her hand to her ear . . . and welcomed a loud yessss, followed by one wise guy who said, 'We laugh *at* him.' Chris smiled weakly. Sandy continued,

"Does he make us cry?" A group response to this question was more difficult to anticipate, orchestrate, or draw out, so Sandy was ready. "Here are a couple of comments that have been passed on to me about our Pastor Chris and the subject of crying. I won't read everything, just key passages.

'. . . Pastor Chris's attempts to tell us about his own struggles are so touching that the tears ran down my face that time when he went on and on about–he called it–leveling with you. He was vulnerable and sincere even though some people whispered that it was TMI: too much information . . .'

"And another, '. . . Chris really does care for people who are down and out, but for some reason he doesn't know how or have the forcefulness to follow through on things, like his half-hearted efforts to combat homelessness. At home one evening I got thinking about this sort of thing, and started weeping. It is such a monumental problem and if our minister doesn't really know how to grapple with it, what hope is there?'"

The place went dead quiet. Sandy gasped, "Yeah, that was heavy," and turned to Chris, "'You taught us to make living funerals into roasts as well as toasts. Right?"

Head down and looking serious, he nodded.

Then she said, "Here's another question to ask if you want to find out how a minister is doing: Does he make them–us–feel religious." She looked over at Chris who had the start of a grin. She said, "I think he's going to laugh!" Then Paige started a chant that they all picked up on:

"We are religious! We are religious! We are religious!"

Chris joined in with the rest of them, but when the chanting had run its course, he called out: "Or not!" and the rest of them joined in: "Or not! Or not! Or not!"

Gloria said, "Chris taught us to say those two words following any overly confident pronouncement we make. It brings us back to earth."

Pastor Ek, energized by both the upbeat mood and brutal candor, shot back at Gloria, "Why do we need to come back to earth? What's wrong with heaven? Like the golf course?"

No response came to this one that Chris thought was timely and funny. Sandy smiled at him and said, "I'm almost done here, but I want to share something that I told Pastor during his first week on the job when he asked what has worked in the past to make life better for new Meadows clergy. I told him, 'Make sure that we have sparkling clean rest rooms and nurseries.' Looking out at the congregation she asked, expecting broad affirmation, "Has he succeeded? On this one? Overall?'"

Heads moved in all directions. One woman held her nose. Another thought, "*These comments: 'We are religious and Or Not' border on sacrilege. I take religion more seriously than this minister. What is he teaching our kids?*"

Ebby Stone jumped up, resumed an emcee role, and asked for another round of applause for Sandy. Then he signaled Joyce to say something. Nobody expected her words to maintain the energy that had charged the room so far, but they were ready to listen. Joyce seldom spoke to large groups of adults. She was a deeds person. Not words. She began very seriously.

"I have a brother-in-law called John who is an experienced Lutheran minister. I dearly respect him and treasure his advice. Before Chris began at Meadows I emailed John asking him to share any advice he could offer that might turn out to be helpful to new pastors.

"He replied right away saying 'Preach good sermons, visit people who are ill or troubled, and show members that you love them. Not simply endure them, love them. All other mistakes and inadequacies are forgiven or overlooked if these things are in place.'

"All other things?" I asked him.

"'Of course, there can be egregious wrongs like misuse of funds or abuse of children, but what I have in mind are crises that can fester if the pastor is unable to cope, or if he becomes controversial in a negative sense. Like wanting to remove the American flag from the sanctuary (A delicate matter which can upset veterans), like not being patient with back slappers, like not addressing complaints from parents about their kid in a youth-study class, or not being able to identify with the sports passions of members.'

"John ended this bit of advice by saying, 'Seriously, I have met some young ministers who told me that they would trade their Phi Beta Kappa keys for being able to do golf.'

"Believe me," said Joyce. "My friend Pastor John did not know about Chris's golf compulsion when he said that. So, what do I come away with having crossed paths with one Reverend Ek? Welllllll . . .," she said before a long pause, "I will miss him greatly and will find it very hard to define what we want from our next pastor without saying, do it like Chris. I have come to so respect and admire the guy. What he has done with our youth is so amazing, and he never expects credit. I'm going to leave it at that. Those of you who know me know that I'm not much with testimonials, but I want you to remember this: I have come to almost worship Chris Ek."

Everything stayed quiet as Joyce took her seat. Ebby Stone acted like he didn't know what to do next until Gloria got his attention and pointed at Paige who came to the front with what appeared to be several pages of notes. She fiddled with them on the lectern, adjusted her glasses so they slid to the end of her nose, sipped from a water bottle, and cleared her throat. Two older members rolled their eyes. Paige had everyone's attention, and she knew it. Without any small talk or attempt to be funny, she said,

"Our pastor has grown during his time with us, and if his thoughts and behaviors continue to evolve, that is a good thing. They are asked to do so many things by congregations like ours–the pastors–that I wonder if a lifetime is enough to get control of everything. Maybe we should give these people lifetime appointments. Then we can legitimately expect them to come close to being our miracle workers and take the monkeys off their backs–those creatures like us who claw and nip and chatter endlessly . . ."

Paige momentarily lost track of where she was supposed to be in her notes, which led to an unplanned pause. One person in the back clapped and the rest joined in to create a full-throated amen. She interpreted it as a sign of support for her: Her personhood. Her leadership. Her precocity. When she found her place again her confidence and voice were full.

". . . I suppose one question becomes 'With whom does the pastor share his thoughts as he grows? In this church Chris Ek has shared with us, his youngest charges. He describes the essence of that growth as honesty being the best policy, even in religion . . . [Paige paused. She had anticipated some audience reaction here, but they stayed quiet.] . . . and Pastor Chris has been honest with us. We are so grateful for it. Right? [She looked at her classmates who nodded.] Let's be very clear on my next point: our pastor is not leaving this job because he has done anything wrong like he has lost his faith or stolen money or buggered the bursar. He is off to learn more in a faraway place that will challenge him to think and do."

Joyce Ahlgren dropped her head and held it in her hands *"and I raised this kid? Who does she think she is?"*

Joyce's daughter continued, "Humbly, I say he has changed this place through his indirect influence on families. He has quietly and relentlessly empowered us kids, and he has raised the expectations that our families have for us. He has brought us to the age of majority before our time. We have become teachers of our parents. They are learners along with us. Now Chris will say that he is the learner and we are his teachers, and that may be somewhat true, but when people learn things without even realizing it, that is powerful. We know that subtle racism and sexism and xenophobia can creep up on us without being detected, but those are other stories which I will not go into here."

Someone clapped. Another shushed him. Paige continued as if she didn't hear. "I don't think any of us in the church will fully realize what this man has done for us until he is long gone.

"And it's not just for us kids. It's inter-generational. Let me share an example. A few months ago, we did an apple pie fund-raiser to help us go to a national youth gathering. We had no clue how to make an apple pie at the start, let alone a bunch of them to sell, at least I didn't. You old ladies out there helped us figure out ingredients, roll dough from scratch, and bake them in the church kitchen. I learned so much from you, and I am told that you all got to know us better. Right? A functioning youth group cannot realize full success unless it works with a–what should I call it–old people's group. Chris let it happen. He made it happen."

A smattering of applause.

Looking over at Chris, Paige said, "As I understand it, a big challenge you ministers have is criticism from parents who think you aren't doing enough for their kid, connecting with them or whatever. Like the minister can have a calendar full of activities for the youth, but if *their* kid isn't in-volved or doesn't want to be involved, it's somehow the pastor's fault. Well, let me say this publicly: I have never heard this complaint from parents at our church, and let me ask you all this right now: Have any of you thought that this guy didn't give his all to your kids? Or to all of us kids? Have you?"

"Noooo," came the response to Paige's call. She paused, straightened her papers, looked her congregation in the eye, and said,

"I have had a little bit of experience this year with homeless people. To most of society they are faceless and nameless, but each one of them has a life and a story. I have seen Jesus and myself in them and many times feel moved after spending time with them. They have so much to give. Many churches, including Meadows, like to write out checks or host these people for a week. They don't want to get any more involved than that. They don't want to get their hands dirty. But human contact with people who are homeless can take you and me to places within human hearts. The problem is we don't want to be uncomfortable, yet we need discomfort to see the work of God. The homeless can make us uncomfortable, but we can see God in them and their struggles, and perhaps most importantly in what they have to offer us."

Paige was on a roll and could have gone on forever, but she sensed uneasiness in the pews and closed with this burst. "As a beginning golfer, I have learned so much from Mr. Keyshawn Gentry. He's sitting right there in case you don't know him. [She pointed] He emphasizes the importance of how we hold the club. A sound grip, he calls it. A sound grip as a foundation for hitting the ball far and straight. You have to learn how firm or light to hold it. Hands opposed. Knuckles in the correct position. A good grip is inerrant scripture. Right, Mr. Gentry?"

He nodded.

"Well," concluded Paige, "Also with the ministry the grip is key. If I–she moved into the first person–run things like a tyrant thinking I know it all and squeeze the club to death, I get nowhere. If I loosen the grip and listen, and invite others to be involved, we all learn. Enough said."

She was done and sat down. The response from the congregation was resounding silence.

Gloria asked Paige to stand again, and thanked her profusely. "You are our leader, Paige. Sometimes, you are one (ahem) tough broad, and I wouldn't want to be pitted against you, but I love you. We all love you."

The congregation sprang to their feet and gave a long ovation to the kids and their minister. Then Gloria said, "We're almost done." The lights were turned down as the kids formed a half circle at the front. Gloria lit a long white candle. On the piano Mary Beth softly played the melody they were about to sing, and Gloria said, "Please hum along." The students crooned in simple harmony:

> Fair are the meadows, fairer still the woodlands,
>
> Robed in the blooming garb of spring;
>
> May light shine brighter, where ere you wander,
>
> Our love will follow on birds' wings.

Chris's service was over. Gloria called out, "Please stay for refreshments in the Riley Room."

Eberhard Stone and Joyce Ahlgren were standing together sipping coffee with Mrs. Snyder as he said, "They love him, but they also realize that he is clearly quite a guy, and his right-hand man–woman–is Paige. She is so different from him, but he has turned her loose. And they collide. Right, Joyce?"

Paige's mother was starting to blush and kept quiet.

"Yep," Stone continued. "That daughter of yours reminds myself of me when I was . . . well, she reminds me of me. Enough said."

Epilog

A Message from Durban, South Africa

"Dear friends in Christ,

"I apologize for taking so long to get back to you. Things are hectic here, and I'm still working into a schedule that will leave time for correspondence with pals like you back home. I must say this though: I will not be using electronic media: Face Time, Skype, email, texting, or any of those other truly miraculous ways of staying in touch immediately. I'm committed to communicating the old-fashioned way: snail mail, but that's a misnomer because I can't send anything–like a physical letter–from South Africa to you and avoid air mail. I want you to feel close to me by handling the same paper that I have written on, and I want to back off from the pre-occupation of always being in the now with breathlessly important things to say. News and thinking can take their good old sweet times with me. So often what at the moment seems like it must be attended to right away, turns out to be just another bump in the road when we look back at it week or year or lifetime later. We need perspective and separation from what is so compulsively *now*. Anyway, I do.

"Let me give you an example that has boosted me up onto this high horse. I know from my contacts back in Belle Waters that high schoolers sponsored as Rotary International students are discouraged from encouraging visits by their families or friends while they are abroad, the purpose being to force them into relying on new resources and relationships. Makes sense, right? Well, while the no visits bit is usually honored, social media messages flash back and forth every day between continents at the speed of light. So, the Rotary international students *are* in touch with the folks back home, maybe even more than when they lived Stateside. Not that that's bad, necessarily, but learning to be independent from home and empathetic toward new cultures can be diminished by constant contacts with our old comfort zones. So, please think of me as a Rotary student abroad, let's say circa 1967, who is going to try hard to learn from new experiences and who loves to get letters I can hold.

"I never gave a sermon about living abroad when I was at Meadows, but if I did it might have gone like this: journeys are built into our aspirations. Our stories, the great ones like The Exodus, the Odyssey, global circumnavigation, space travel, and the small ones like golf, reveal our restlessness. We gotta get somewhere! Even clergy (especially clergy?) can become pre-occupied with moving on. I mentioned this inclination in my very first sermon to you back in Belle Waters. (Good grief, before even formally taking the job at Meadows I was thinking of moving on.) Some denominations make the moving on decisions top-down directed by their hierarchy with minimal input from the man or woman in the pulpit who is going to be uprooted. (I call these souls tumbleweeds.) Thank goodness, congregational churches like Meadows try to make such decisions on site when the time is right for everyone.

"So, I have to ask, did I leave you too soon? That question tugged at my heart during the fabulous funeral service for me. For the rest of that day I wished I could have taken back my decision to move on. The kids were so generous and sweet about my time with them. I slept fitfully that night, but by the morning I once more felt like the Peace Corps is the answer. As I look back from half a world away, it has been a good move so far, but time will tell. Remember this: I am not giving up on the ministry. I will be back, somewhere.

"In the meantime, let me share a couple of things that have stuck with me from Meadows, beyond their moment. If you are like me, some words stay in your memories long after they are said. I will always remember Paige's comments when she argued for taking monkeys off the backs of clergy who are expected to do everything. She called them–the monkeys–creatures like members who claw and nip and chatter endlessly. Well, dear friends of Meadows, there are real monkeys here in Durban who do those very things. Like many newcomers, at first I thought they were cute, and I guess they are, but they hurt–the bites–a little bit at first but then I realize that the fascinating creatures are just being themselves, and I should try to understand them better. They are baboons, the ones that I have encountered. They use at least ten unique vocalizations to communicate with members of their troop. Not dummies, these monkeys, and they can draw blood.

"I don't know what you all think about when you hear the words South Africa, but if you are like most people you probably don't think of

Indians–like people from India–but they have played an important role here. Mahatma Gandhi is the most prominent one. I'm starting to learn more about this man who was the main leader of the Indian national independence movement away from Britain, but who spent twenty years in South Africa and is revered as a leader of civil rights struggles here. Indians, like South African 'blacks' and 'coloreds,' suffered from the apartheid policies of the governing minority white governments. Gandhi experienced discrimination, beatings, jailings, and other indignities that turned him in to a non-violent social activist, idolized by the world.

"However, the Gandhi who lived in South Africa from 1893 to 1914 and who has been judged by me–along with Jesus, Martin Luther King, Mother Teresa, Albert Schweitzer, and Joyce Ahlgren–as a saint, has his harsh critics. I didn't realize this before coming here. These people say that Gandhi kept the struggle of Indians in South Africa separate from that of the lower status blacks and coloreds, and it resulted in him being indifferent to the plights of the other groups who were dispossessed. Sometimes Gandhi even used the word 'Kaffir'–think our N-word–for blacks in South Africa.

"Here's my point: when I realized this, I thought back to you dear Meadows people and others who try to do something about homelessness. You have critics like Robert Lupton, that author of *Toxic Charity* and Paige (Are you reading this, Ms Ahlgren?) who hold your feet and mine to the fire about the real motives in helping the homeless. Please listen to them, *but please also stick with your ongoing efforts however imperfect they may be. Don't be discouraged. Don't give up on Hands!*

"I could go on and on. Here's a bit about the Peace Corps job: When I try to teach English to my kids, I require that they try to teach me something in return. Something in one of their languages. Get this. South Africa has eleven official languages. I can now write down their names from memory: Afrikaans, English, Ndebele, Northern Sotho, Sotho, Swazi, Tsonga, Tswana, Venda, Xhosa and Zulu. I know from a visit to the national parliament in Cape Town that legislators often start out speaking in one language, and then switch to a second or third or more in order to empathize with the linguistic diversity of the country. The accompanying switch in tone and cadence has a beauty that I have observed in American Catholic churches that switch back and forth from Latin to English, and more recently with courageous attempts at back and forth presentations in Spanish and English in Belle Waters.

"Well, you all know that I subscribe to the maxim that when we teach, we learn. I want my South African pupils to taste that salty bit of truth and at the same time I want to move out of my ocean of English into other waters. (If I were totally candid with them I would share the fact that I want to learn

Afrikaans, but since it is so linked to the apartheid past, I'm going to have to pick up that one from somewhere other than my classes.) Since I am living in KwaZulu-Natal, I easily fell into favoring Zulu. My default starting sentence so far has been 'I am from Belle Waters, Wisconsin USA. Tell me where you are from in Zulu.' Most of them reply, 'Ngitshele lapho ukhona kusukela ngesiZulu.'

"We quickly get to more serious subjects: One said to me, 'I want to communicate the following Zulu sentence in English: Kungani neMelika babe izigqila abamnyama? Ngingakwati yini Kuba sakhamuti egcwele uma mina ngivele ngeza la Wisconsin?' (Why did America have black slaves? Could I be a full citizen if I came to Wisconsin?)

"This setting is so stimulating. It reminds me of my days in the south side of Chicago where I got to know two South African boys with whom I still communicate, and of course I have great memories of my time with you kids-of-all-ages at Meadows. I certainly learned a lot. I hope you did.

"And then there's golf. You may have heard of South Africans who have had an international impact on the game: Bobbie Locke, Gary Player, Ernie Els, Retief Goosen, Charl Schwartzel, Trevor Immelman, and I'm probably omitting others, but it's Sewsunker 'Papwa' Sewgolum that interests me. He was an Indian who challenged apartheid era practices by taking up golf and succeeding. I won't go into his list of victories here, but it is substantial. I want to introduce my young English learners to his story and caddying. Papwa caddied and learned–and taught–so much. His story is similar to ones that I have encountered among African-Americans who take to golf. Especially, building on their experiences as caddies. In my church ministry, I have tried to combine the inherent attractions of golf with larger values while sharing tales of those who have overcome bias and exclusion. Have I succeeded? I doubt it. It's a work in progress at best. As you may expect, the favorite golfer of my kids here is V.J. Singh, an Indo-Fijian. A great choice. He's such a hard worker and smooth swinger. A member of the World Golf Hall of Fame.

"Starting soon I'm going to try to get my fellow Peace Corps volunteers and others to caddy for some of my kids, and then reverse the role, like we did at Meadows. In the meantime, I have a goal of publicizing the ugly scene of having barbed wire over the fences of some golf courses here.

"Well, I gotta go."

Chris almost wrote the postscript: "*Is Jayne still doing liturgy? I thought she was a natural at it. I never hear from her. Jayne, are you out there? You once said 'I love you,' to me. Carelessly. Right?*" But he didn't, and he drifted deep into thought.

"Was Jayne playing games with me? I have to admit that at times I felt outclassed and manipulated by her, but I liked it. Maybe we aren't (weren't) equals and that stood in our way. An elephant in the room that we could never bring ourselves to talk about. I didn't realize it then. She was probably too polite and nice to bring it up. Looking back, she went from being my caddy, to being my playing partner, to being my golf teacher, along with Keyshawn. She probably could have been my analyst and mother confessor as well, but that could have destroyed our relationship.

"So, what did? Me? Yeah, but I think it was also the failure of the home-lessness proposal. She probably wanted me to bleed and die for that cause. It's ridiculous in this day and age, but we avoided talking about long-term plans together after I gave my LBJ sermon. At the time, I thought she wasn't ready to commit to us–I certainly wasn't–but that may have been the farthest thing from her mind. I hope not, but wouldn't she have said something? Confided in me? Been candid? But, why didn't I? I still have a problem with that sort of thing."

A handwritten note

Jayne propelled the envelope under Chris's office door mid-morning on the day he was scheduled to depart Belle Waters for the Peace Corps, expecting him to be at his desk and see it coming at him like an out of control Jet Ski, but she was too late. He had left the night before. She wrote,

"My great friend Chris,

"I don't know how I'm going to get along without you. I never thought I'd fall for a minister, and I certainly never ex-pected to hook up with a guy who could never beat me in golf. But let me say this: you are more candid and forthcoming than I am and to think that I regularly dissed you for holding back. Bad me. I contradicted my own big-mouthed rhetoric not only by keeping quiet about my golfing past (low handicap, trophies, etc.), but I tricked you more than once which–How can I say this gently–exposed your blatant ignorance of the game in spite of your enthusiasm. You probably are thinking, 'How can she say that about my golf?' or perhaps 'could she be right?' C'mon. Which is it?

"Wellllll, . . . I'm just trying to be candid, but I admit I may be a bit cruel and a fraud. You can take it. Right? Hey, I

*almost peed in my pants that morning I caddied for you. You
really did think I was pathetic, and in a masochistic way, I liked
that. Intense feelings. Finally. From you. You made me feel vulnerable for a change, or maybe faux-vulnerable, I don't know.
And that nine holes we had after your seventy-four that you
bragged about endlessly. . . You were beautifully exposed like all
golfers are for getting so wrapped up in it that you overplayed
your hand: you talked a better game than you played. We all do
it at one time or another. It's hopeful, I guess, to think we can
always be at our best again. Does that apply to our behavior as
practicing church members or Searchers or whatever we hope to
be? I never asked you this. I think it would be a good sermon.*

"So, you were (are?) a challenge for me. A learner. Okay,
we're all learners.

"I really do love you and always will."

"JN"

She had typed his name on the envelope in a gesture of teasing formal-
ity that would suggest to most people that this contains a mass-produced
legal document. When she assertively slid it under Chris's door, instead
of skimming across the floor toward his desk, it lodged beneath the green
piece of carpet he had laid down as a putting surface. When the interim
pastor who succeeded Chris cleaned up his space to make it hers weeks later,
she sighed, sneezed, chuckled, and recycled it. Unopened.

Breaking His Vow

Chris meant it when he said he intended to communicate with his flock
back at Meadows only via slow mail. He vowed he would stick to this commitment "no matter what" and encouraged others to respond in kind. Many
members still wrote in this painstakingly inefficient way. His young friends
tried but couldn't bear to do it every time.

He kept his word for a long time, but finally cracked after Paige texted
him desperately looking for a prayer in ten words or fewer that she would
share at what she said was an important gathering. "Please I need it right
away, like today, Pastor Chris. Can't you send me something that meets
this length requirement while telling the truth profoundly?" And then she
added one of those smiling faces.

Chris wanted to help her, and breaking his vow was not a big deal in this instance. He decided to share something that had become very important to him. It read, "Dear God, I am doing the best I can." He attributed it to Huston Smith, a scholar of religion who said it was his favorite prayer. It came from a nine-year-old boy whose mother had found it scribbled on a piece of paper near his bed.

Chris texted it off. Ten minutes later Paige replied via email with profuse thanks, an editorial addendum, and news. She said,

"I will be adding *or not* at the end. Along with amen, of course.

"And a couple of more things: Sharon and I have been putting together another proposal, this one to be sent to the Belle Waters School Board. We want to start a charter school called 7/11 (Or 7:11 or Seven Eleven, whatever). That's 24:00 minus 16:49, or the time we spend in school. It will be hypersensitive to the perspective of homeless kids. We will build on their street smarts and survival skills and tie it into the entrepreneurship program at Belle Waters College (although I have not talked to them yet). Our school's board must have some members who have spent some time on the streets, along with some ongoing homeless students. We will make the curriculum rigorous and be sure to address the usual Department of Public Instruction standards. What do you think, oh my esteemed guru, pastor, guide, and teacher (and student . . .? I couldn't resist!)? Does it have a chance?

"By the way, Keyshawn, Alan, and Carleton now attend Meadows regularly. So does Sharon. We go together. I don't know where Jayne is or what she's up to.

"But, I'm saving the best until last. It's another miracle, like yours . . . I got a hole-in-one yesterday. What do you think it means?"

Discussion Questions

For Members

How courageous can our clergy be in presenting new overtures to our membership?

How careful must they be?

How far should a church go in addressing social issues?

How much personal freedom should a clergy person have in his/her behavior "off the clock"?

To what extent is it possible for a clergy person to be off the clock? . . . Not expected to be on call for parishioners at all times?

What role do sports play in the messages and values of your church?

While the golfing culture of Fair Are the Meadows church in the book may seem far-fetched, how might some of the golfing axioms apply? In other sports? in the arts? the sciences? technology? something else?

How has your congregation been affected by competing events such as Sunday morning soccer practice, NFL games on noon television, or something else?

What are examples of good (and bad) behavior coming from sports that have affected your congregation?

How does your congregation address homelessness? Have you had candid conversations about your church's relationship to homeless people?

How do you react to Paige in the book? Jane? Chris? Sharon? Mrs. Ahlgren?

Is Paige like young Jesus?

What have you learned about keeping your young people active . . .?

. . . from very early ages?

. . . after confirmation?

How do you learn about your potential ministers before calling them?

How important is musical sensitivity in your minister?

What is off-limits regarding ministerial behavior?

To what extent are the highs and lows of golf (or any sport) a metaphor for life?

To what extent is your congregation aware of the snobbery that can accompany attachment to a particular sport like golf, or something else like the arts, intellectual life, or trending culture?

To what extent does your minister "tell it like it is" from the pulpit? That is, say the same sort of thing in different settings like discussion groups or in a social setting with seminary pals?

To what extent do you wish your congregation could do what other congregations are doing?

How candid should you be in evaluating your minister?

What blind spots might you have regarding the role of your pastor?

What is the role of confidentiality in your relationship with your pastor?

How seriously should you take the values and behavior of your young people?

Are there any limits on the relationships your clergy can have with others? Does it matter if the others are members of your congregation?

For Clergy

How courageous can I be in presenting overtures to our membership?

How careful must I be?

What do you know about your congregation now that you wish you had known before taking the job?

To what extent has *your age* been a factor in how your congregation reacts to you? Do they see you as too young? Too old? Similarly, your gender? Your sexual orientation? Your social-economic background?

What are examples of words or deeds by members that help you do your job?

What are examples of unwitting or sub-consciously motivated words or deeds by members that stand in the way of your full commitment to your call? Or that really hurt?

How important is musical sensitivity in your congregation?

Are there particular demographic groups that you feel especially comfortable (or uncomfortable) serving?

How candid should you be in evaluating your congregation?

What blind spots might you have regarding your job or congregation?

What is the role of confidentiality in your relationship with your congregation?

To what extent are the children in Fair Are the Meadows Church like young Jesus?

Acknowledgements

I owe many thanks to pre-publication readers and others.

The feedback from several non-golfing ordained ministers was critical as I tried to bring to life the agonies and joys of their vocation. Theologian Arland Hultgren helped me with Biblical passages and some finer points of getting and keeping a ministerial job. Rev. Stephen Hawkins shared his perspective as a youthful, new pastor. Heather Hultgren–and her daughter, Valerie–helped me learn from the perspectives of young people.

Golfing clergy played an important role, especially Steve Howland, and Jamie Geiger. Arvid Adell, Denver Bitner, Rick Meier, Jerry Peterson, Loren Nielsen, and Mike Thomas provided helpful questions along with laypersons Webbs Norman, Geri Nickolai, Steve Stark, David Sanders, and Chuck Benedict.

My life-long golfing pals Jim Carlson, Bill Stark, and Ron Adamson were there to read and refine my musings about the game.

Robin Stuht, Jeff Hoyt, and Bitner shared insights and resources for addressing the needs of homeless people.

Darrah Chavey and Carol Taylor kept religious humor coming at me. David Heesen provided helpful proofreading. Mark Spreitzer and Mardie Farr and were co-operative models for a photographic image of two of the book's main characters.

Jerry Gustafson, Henry Kisor, Hawkins, Howland, Geiger, and the Hultgrens closely read my developing manuscripts, and responded with helpful, valuable input. I greatly enjoyed the comments back and forth with them and with Anna Marie Benander, my most demanding critic and cornucopia of ideas.

The Learner *is a book of fiction. Except for some details drawn from Beloit, Wisconsin, and Zion Lutheran Church in Rockford, Illinois, it is the product of my imagination and experience.*